1988
1ST

228

BOB
NEWHART

BOB NEWHART

JEFF
SORENSEN

ST. MARTIN'S PRESS
NEW YORK

BOB NEWHART. Copyright © 1988 by Jeff Sorensen. All rights reserved.
Printed in the United States of America. No part of this book may be used
or reproduced in any manner whatsoever without written permission except
in the case of brief quotations embodied in critical articles or reviews. For
information, address St. Martin's Press, 175 Fifth Avenue, New York, N.Y.
10010.

Design by Jessica Shatan

Library of Congress Cataloging-in-Publication Data

Sorenson, Jeff.
    Bob Newhart / by Jeff Sorenson.
       p.   cm.
    ISBN 0-312-01741-3
    1. Newhart, Bob. 2. Comedians—United States—Biography.
    3. Television actors and actresses—United States—Biography.
    I. Title.
    PN2287.N43S6 1988
    792.7'028'0924—dc 19   87-38248
    [B]   CIP

First Edition

10 9 8 7 6 5 4 3 2 1

CONTENTS

1 | THE MASTER OF MELLOW

Bob Newhart works in slow motion. His pauses and long-delayed reactions are what make him such a fine comedian. He's got the ability to ride out a few seconds of silence, then with a slight wince or stammer, or maybe just a dart of the eyes, get more of a laugh than other comedians get with a whole series of witty, well-turned remarks. His style is perfect for television: in close-ups, viewers get to savor all of those slightly raised eyebrows and subtle expressions.

He's so good at what he does that he has remained one of America's best-loved comedians for the past twenty-five years. And he has succeeded in becoming the star of two hit sitcoms ("The Bob Newhart Show" and "Newhart"), a feat that nobody else has managed in decades. As a reviewer for *The New York Times* once said about Newhart's current series, "Comic fashions may come and go with the thirteen-week season, but Mr. Newhart seems to be timeless."

When asked how he explains his long record of popular successes, Newhart answers, "I guess the American public doesn't feel threatened by me." When Newhart gives this kind of response, it's mostly an example of his playing the part of a terribly modest guy who can't believe that people admire him. On the other hand, there is a certain amount of truth in his remark: Newhart certainly doesn't present a very threatening image. (Anybody who feels intimidated by Bob Hartley or Dick Loudon, the characters he portrays in his situation comedies, would probably find Mr. Rogers intimidating.) Instead, he's the sort of person we can feel comfortable spending time with.

Newhart usually plays the part of a levelheaded, fairly ordinary guy reacting incredulously to all the craziness going on around him. (For that reason, the role of Bob Hartley, a psychologist, on "The Bob Newhart Show" was ideal for him.) Newhart says he gets laughs from "listening to people and having to be nice to them no matter what they do." It all sounds so easy—and yet, how many other actors are able to get as much comic mileage out of a simple blink of the eyes or a stammer? In fact, his funniest lines often consist of him saying "uhuh" or "right" or "I see"; it all comes down to his unique talent for reacting to things in amusing ways.

Here is a typical Newhart moment (from the old sitcom, "The Bob Newhart Show"): An extraordinarily good-looking, well-built tennis pro, with an ego the size of his biceps, is talking to Bob Hartley. "You have no idea," the tennis pro says, "of the problems that we incredibly handsome people have to face." Bob thinks for a few seconds and then, with a look of total resignation, answers, "No, I suppose not."

Of course, an important part of why a joke like this works is because Newhart has the sort of face that couldn't be described as that of a matinee idol. "The truth is," he admits, "I look like an accountant." (And Newhart actually did work as an accountant for several years.)

Another typical Newhart scene involves Dick Loudon, the innkeeper he plays in the current sitcom, and his handyman, George Utley. Dick and George are sitting across from each other at a table in the dining room of the inn. In a loud voice, George says, "Dick, my paycheck bounced." All the guests who are in the dining room immediately turn their heads and look at Dick, who's clearly feeling highly uncomfortable. Dick leans back in his chair and cringes with embarrassment. He then tries to manage a smile, laughs weakly, stammers a little, and says, "Obviously a bank error." Dick makes a good try, but it's clear that everyone in the place is convinced he is bankrupt.

Newhart says that when he was growing up, he was a big fan of Jack Benny's, and it's certain that Newhart picked up a lot of what he knows about comedy from him. "Just listening to him on the radio, I learned about timing," explains Newhart. Jack was utterly fearless. . . . He could take all the time he wanted to, because he knew the joke would always pay off."

The Benny influence is apparent in much of Newhart's acting. Take this scene from "The Bob Newhart Show": Emily has bought a terribly expensive watch for Bob on his birthday, and when he finds out, he's shocked that she could have spent the money so foolishly.

BOB: Emily, I wouldn't mind if you had spent thirteen hundred dollars on a piano. I mean, because a twenty-dollar piano is no good. But a twenty-dollar watch will do the same thing *that* watch does . . . and with the money left over . . . Well, you could buy a piano. . . . Then you'd have a piano and a watch . . . for the price of that watch.

EMILY: You know, Bob, I never realized it before—you're cheap.

BOB: For somebody who's cheap, I'm wearing a pretty expensive watch.

What reminds us of Jack Benny is a scene like this is more than just that Bob Hartley is cheap. It has to do with the way Newhart, like Benny, draws out his lines with lots of pauses and reactions, making us feel that his character is really thinking up what he is saying and not just reciting from a script. Bob Hartley talks like a person out of real life.

Another key point about Newhart's brand of humor is that it is understated. His shows make a point of avoiding slapstick, gratuitous insult jokes, and—especially—clever remarks that are put into the mouths of precocious children.

Newhart explains that the secret of being truly funny is "saying things in the fewest number of words and giving the audience some credit for being able to figure it out." In his stand-up routines, for instance, we hear only his half of a telephone conversation, and "the audience isn't laughing at you, they're laughing at being smart enough to figure it out. . . . They're supplying the information."

One of his cleverest stand-up routines, "Abe Lincoln versus Madison Avenue," is a good example of Newhart's comedy. The premise of this bit is that Newhart considers what would have happened if the art of public relations had been as highly developed in Abraham Lincoln's time as it is today. Newhart suggests that if a man like Lincoln hadn't existed, the image makers would have had to have created him. In the routine, Newhart imagines a phone conversation between a PR man in Washington and Lincoln in Gettysburg. The PR man is disturbed to hear that Lincoln has rewritten the speech his staff has prepared for him to deliver: "You changed 'four score and seven' to what? . . . to eighty-seven? . . . I understand it means the same thing, Abe, but it's supposed to be a *grabber*. We test-marketed 'four score and seven' in Erie and they flipped."

Says Newhart, "That Abe Lincoln routine is not funny on a piece of paper. It's what isn't said that's funny. None of what the PR guy says is funny. It's what Abe says."

Characteristically, Newhart says there's nothing particularly difficult involved in writing and performing his comic routines. "You ask a question, you allow enough time for the person to answer, and then you repeat it," he explains. "How else could you do it?" (Sometimes Newhart can be almost maddeningly humble; surely he can't really believe that anyone could do what he does.)

Just like his stand-up routines, Newhart's situation comedies are designed for an audience with a certain measure of intelligence. Most TV series—whether they're cop shows filled with nonstop action or comedies filled with inane wisecracks—seem to be created for viewers with the attention span of a hyperactive child. But Newhart's sitcoms aim to be different. For viewers who want something a little more subtle, his shows are an oasis of sophistication in the TV schedule.

Newhart explains, "I think that if we do anything, we compliment the audience by saying, 'We think that you have the intelligence to understand this joke. So we're not going to hit you over the head with it.' This usually elicits a perfectly good response, because they realize they're being complimented. When I was off TV, people would ask me to please come back—which I think was their way of saying, 'There's nothing out there for us.'"

He says that he has a very clear idea of the sort of viewer he feels he typically reaches. "They're thirty-five to forty, college graduates, second marriage, a Mercedes and a station wagon, one kid from the first marriage, two from the second." Newhart believes that his series tend to have an older audience than most sitcoms. "Our show ["Newhart"] is radical in that it's based on the premise that two adults can actually solve their own problems without the aid of their children coming in at the last minute."

Newhart insists that his job in the sitcoms is really quite simple: his only technique, he says, is to play himself. "I always play Bob Newhart—and I'm very comfortable playing Bob Newhart. I realize I'm not in the same league with these fellas, but Spencer Tracy and Cary Grant were great, and they always played Spencer Tracy and Cary Grant."

And Newhart has no plans to change his style. "No, let's be honest," he explains. "I am what I am. I mean, if I tried to perform in a Western as a gunslinger with a big hat and spurs, and I walked through the barroom door and growled, 'Where's Mike?' the audience would burst into laughter. Seriously, I'm not gonna change just for the sake of change.

"Keep in mind, when I started in the late fifties, I didn't say to myself, 'Oh, here's a great void to fill—I'll be a balding exaccountant who specializes in low-key humor.' That's simply what I was and that's the direction my mind always went in, so it was natural for me to be that way."

How much does the real Bob Newhart have in common with the characters he plays? Quite a bit, say those who have worked with him—although Newhart does seem to be a little more driven and anxious than Dick Loudon or Bob Hartley. Newhart chain-smokes, for instance, and he becomes extremely tense before a performance.

"Our personalities show up pretty well on stage, and privately Bob is low-keyed and laid-back the way you see him as a performer," says comedian Don Rickles, a good friend of Newhart's for many years. "But nobody could be more concerned about his work than Bob. Every comedian has one attitude; his is that of the stammering, groping modern man. He works very hard to maintain that attitude."

Steven Kampmann, who played Kirk Devane on "Newhart," wonders, "If he's so low-key, why does he chain-smoke? I think maybe there's another side to him. I'm looking forward to seeing it!"

Michael Zinberg, the executive producer of "The Bob Newhart Show," explains that "Bob is not a saint. He's got a temper. He has a tight act and has a compulsion to be funny. . . . I'm sure his anxieties began on the saloon circuit, with the terrible hours and getting so wound up. Those years took a lot out of him."

Although Newhart describes himself as "a relatively easygoing person," he admits that "being in show business tends to make you nervous. You know that you're gonna be seen by millions on TV, and that alone gives you tension. And when you're out on a nightclub floor, you know you have to make people laugh each and every performance.

"There's no drug in the world as depressing as a routine that doesn't work," explains Newhart. And he says that bombing in front of an audience is such a traumatic experience for him that he can still remember, nearly word for word, all of his stand-up routines and sitcom episodes that have failed to get laughs. The deafening silence of an unamused audience is, for Newhart, the ultimate form of torture.

Newhart loves to hear applause, but he is uneasy with the fame that goes along with starring in a hit TV show. He says that one of the biggest problems for a comedian is that people expect him to be funny all the time. For that reason, Newhart usually avoids going to social gatherings. "I have known comedians who have worked up all kinds of comedy routines for parties so that people will say how wonderful they are. Comedy under those conditions becomes a compulsion, a sickness. I would rather be a social failure."

Several of those who have worked with him on TV say that having a conversation with Newhart off camera can be an unusual, even a surreal, experience. In real life, Newhart pauses and stammers in almost exactly the same way that his characters on television do. Naturally, this causes some confusion. Even if he's just asking "How are you?" people wonder if Newhart is doing something from one of his comedy routines. Jennifer Holmes, who played Leslie Venderkellen, the maid from the first season of "Newhart," explains, "He talks in that dry, quiet, little voice, and you keep straining for the joke so you'll be sure to laugh—only you don't hear it. And then you think, I must have missed it; he'll think I'm dumb."

Every few years, it seems, the grind of performing regularly gets to be too much for Newhart, and he decides to take some time off to relax, play a lot of golf (a Newhart obsession), and be with his family. When he does this, there are inevitably those who accuse him of being, shall we say, less industrious than he might be. Robert Wussler, then the president of CBS-TV, said in 1978 (after Newhart had decided to stop doing "The Bob Newhart Show," "He'd rather play golf three hundred sixty-five days a year than continue acting." Newhart says he's still a bit irritated by Wussler's comment. "What I actually said was, 'I've heard it's boring to play golf three hundred sixty-five days a year, but I'd like to find out for myself.'"

Still, Newhart usually isn't able to stay inactive for long. He says he was beginning to feel restless a few years ago, and that's when he decided to put together another sitcom, "Newhart." "You have to put yourself up against challenges," he explains. "That's what life is." And Newhart's fans are certainly grateful that he has put down his golf clubs often enough over the past twenty-five years to give us some truly entertaining comedy series and albums.

2

"I WONDER HOW I EVER GOT TO BE A COMIC"

Most comedians are misfits. While growing up they are usually rebels or social outcasts of one kind or another. They remember years of attempting to overcome the obstacles of poverty, discrimination, or just the stigma of being somehow different from everybody else.

Not so with Bob Newhart. His early years appear, at least on the surface, to be full of the same experiences as those of any ordinary middle-class fellow. By his late twenties it might have seemed a safe bet that Newhart had finally settled down to a humdrum life as an accountant with a Chicago firm. What's more, he even *looked* like an accountant: his hairline was already receding before his thirtieth birthday. Most of Newhart's co-workers had no idea that this taciturn guy who did his job diligently was also gifted with a quick wit and an inventive imagination.

Not even Newhart understands why he didn't fit into the mold of most of his contemporaries. "Sometimes I wonder how I ever got to be a comic," says Newhart. "I didn't come from a broken home, so I'm not trying to get away from my drab and unhappy home life by retreating within myself and only coming out to poke fun at other people to turn their scorn from me. I wasn't an odd-looking kid that everybody made fun of, so I'm not battling ridicule directed at me back at others in self-defense—which is usually the way a comic gets wound up."

Bob Newhart was born on September 5, 1929, and he was christened George Robert Newhart. (His father was also named George, so in order to avoid confusion at home, the boy was always called Bob.) Bob has three sisters—Virginia, Mary Joan, and Pauline; Mary Joan is a nun who has taught at a Chicago high school. Bob was the second-born of the four children. His father was part-owner of a plumbing and heating-supply business. Bob's mother, Pauline, was a housewife. He grew up in this fairly typical middle-American family, and they lived on the far West Side of Chicago. Bob describes his family as warm and close-knit and says his childhood was "neither more nor less hilarious than anyone else's."

Jack Spatafora, who knew Bob Newhart well throughout the 1950s, says, "Yes, Bob came from a very atypical background for a comedian—a quiet, middle-class, Irish-Catholic family in the suburban areas of Chicago. . . . Bob's life was always fairly comfortable, never rich or anything, but he never had to go through any real suffering. So as a result his humor is much gentler, much less angry and less full of a sense of being out to change the world than many of the other comedians."

Newhart was educated at Catholic schools in the Chicago area, and this background played an important role in forming his character. His early schooling was fairly strict and rigid—even holding hands with a girl in public was considered a little risqué. ("I'm just now getting out of that guilt bag," explains Newhart.) So it's not surprising that Bob developed into a polite, well-behaved young man. He was not one to be found pulling pranks or telling dirty stories.

Says Jack White, who first met Newhart when they were about twelve years old, "We both went to St. Catherine's Grammar School, St. Ignatius High School, and Loyola University. . . . There weren't too many fellows from our neighborhood who traveled to the center of the city to go to St. Ignatius, and that's how I got to know him—we both went back and forth on the streetcars.

"Bob was always a very genuine guy, very bright and interesting to talk to. He always walked a bit to the tune of his own drummer. He seemed to be quite inner-directed: Bob really didn't seem to care about what everybody else was going to do. Wouldn't get caught up in following the crowd the way most kids did.

"He was clever and funny, but he wasn't somebody who

would tell lots of jokes and stories. Wasn't one of those guys who would be the life of the party. Bob had just the average amount of things to say. In high school he wasn't one that you would have pointed to and said, 'He is definitely going to be something tremendous some day.' But yet you wouldn't have ruled it out, either. You wouldn't have said, 'Bob Newhart will never be a big deal.'

"If you were in a class with him, he wasn't one of the people getting the top grades or talking the most, but on the other hand he wouldn't be one of the people who didn't do his work, either. . . . School was not a joke to him. He was a serious student, and he also worked long hours at other jobs. I especially remember that he always had some type of job. Some of us kind of goofed around a lot, but he didn't. He was very organized in using his time."

Newhart remembers that the first time he thought about acting was when he occasionally did impressions of celebrities for his classmates at St. Ignatius. He imitated Humphrey Bogart, James Cagney, Jimmy Durante, Cary Grant, and several others. Newhart says his friends "liked it and I guess that's what started me out. And it was something I enjoyed, too."

Because of his amusing impersonation of Jimmy Durante, Newhart was cast in a production (with an all-male cast, since St. Ignatius was a boys' school) of the play *The Man Who Came to Dinner*. "Bob portrayed the part of Banjo," recalls Tony Mockus, who was also in the production. "And Banjo was played by Jimmy Durante in the movie version. Bob gave a wildly funny characterization; it was terrific and quite different from his subdued style that we're familiar with from TV."

At high school he was also the runner-up in an elocution contest. The winner gave a dramatic reading of Edgar Allen Poe's "Annabel Lee"; Newhart did some of his impressions.

When asked if he was known as one of the class clowns, Newhart replies, "I was never in the center ring putting on hats; I was the guy on the edge of the crowd who said something to the guy next to him who broke up, and then the guy next to *him* said, 'What did he say?' It's always been a laid-back, observational thing. Kind of overheard—it isn't really meant to be heard by anybody."

Newhart has always considered his roots in Chicago to be extremely important to him. He has often gone back to visit and has attended reunions of both his high school and college classmates.

George Avakian, the director of artists and repertory at Warner Brothers Records in the early sixties, comments that "Bob was definitely a very middle-American, very homespun kind of a guy. He never really changed from the way he was when he was back in Chicago. I think that explains why New York nightclubs were not really his sort of thing. And it also explains why television was *exactly* his sort of thing."

"I've always maintained that the easiest audiences to fool were in San Francisco and New York," Newhart says, "because they tend to laugh at what they think they *should* laugh at. You can't fool the people in Chicago because they only laugh if they think it's funny. . . . And it's interesting how many comedians have found success in Chicago, or recognition there, like Shecky Green, myself, Nichols and May, and Shelley Berman. I think Mort Sahl would admit that one of his biggest successes was in Chicago, and Johnny Winters always had a big following there before he hit nationally. There's got to be a reason for that. It can't be a coincidence."

After graduating from St. Ignatius High School in 1947, Newhart enrolled in classes at Loyola University in Chicago. He majored in accounting, and when he received his diploma in 1952, he was awarded the degree of Bachelor of Science in commerce.

Another member of the class of '52 at Loyola, Gene Bertog, remembers, "As strange as it may seem from how things have gone in his later life, Bob wasn't all that well-known or outspoken at the time. People knew who he was, but he was not a class officer or anything like that."

"Bob had a reputation for being the guy who would come up with the quip and find the clever turn of the phrase," explains Jack Spatafora, who also attended Loyola when Newhart was there. "Even as a kid there was something about his poker face that made whatever he had to say funny. And with Bob there was that sly, sardonic twist to his comments. . . . He would say things that other people wouldn't think of."

Those who knew Newhart back in those days say that he used to drink Pepsi-Cola incessantly, almost as if he believed it were the cure for all the diseases known to man.

Jack White recalls, "Bob had the strangest eating habits of anybody. He was absolutely addicted to Pepsi-Cola. I would see him at the student union at Loyola, having breakfast at eight A.M.—and his breakfast would consist of a Pepsi and an atrocious piece of strawberry pie out of a vending machine."

"I taught him in what was called Speech 101, an undergraduate public-speaking course," remembers Mariette Le Blanc. "And he was then very much as he is now—retiring, soft-spoken, and shy. To tell the truth, he didn't like to get up in front of a group of people and talk. . . . But after class there was a group of us that used to congregate down in the student union, and that's where I got to know some of the qualities of Bob Newhart. Because at that time while going through college he was already trying, I think, to write monologues for other comedians to use. He would tell us these stories, and we would all be laughing hysterically, which was a very different experience from when he was up in front of the class giving whatever the speaking assignment was. We would say to him, 'Why don't you try doing these things yourself?' But Bob insisted that he couldn't and he shouldn't and he wouldn't ever do that. . . . He never thought at first that he wanted to perform; he wanted to be a writer instead."

Le Blanc says Newhart never took any dramatics courses, only speech courses. Bertog explains, "Bob and I were in the business school. The 'artsy' people were even on a different campus. They didn't understand us and we sure as hell didn't understand them. So I'm sure that's why Bob wasn't active in the theatrical groups at Loyola."

Newhart was not taking part in any plays at school, but at that time he did join a theatrical club in Oak Park, a suburb of Chicago that borders on the far West Side. Says Spatafora, "He was in a little theater group along with several of us called the Oak Park Playhouse, which was formed around 1950. Bob was in a variety of plays, in different humorous parts. The first play he did was one I remember fondly—I had written a musical comedy version of *Dracula,* and Bob played the part of a hunchbacked butler named Bela.

"What intrigued us about Bob was the fact that we thought

that, despite his obvious abilities, he'd never make it in the theater. We'd always tell him, 'Gee you're funny, Bob, but your humor is meant for a living room.' Everybody in the group thought he was funnier at the cast party after the play than he was on stage. We wondered how he could ever project that humor past the footlights.

"Now the reason we felt that way was because this was the time of the pratfall comedians like Red Skelton and Milton Berle. But as it turned out, by the time Bob was really getting serious about his career, the sit-down type of comedian— which was pioneered by Shelley Berman—really changed the mood of the audience. . . . Sit-down comedy and the close-up cameras on television made it possible for his humor to work. I think that if he had been born five or ten years earlier, he might not have caught on the way he did. Bob came along at exactly the right time."

During the next few years, Newhart continued performing with the Oak Park Playhouse, and Spatafora says that most of his fellow actors and actresses saw him as "one of the lesser lights in the group. We had some very gifted performers in our group, and Bob was probably not one of the most talented as an actor. Even now, Bob's not really a great actor so much as a great *reactor*. And his true forte, I think, is as a writer, a creator of comic situations."

Very soon after graduating from Loyola, Newhart was drafted into the army; he served for two years, from August 1952 until August 1954. However, his only combat experience was with forms and typewriter ribbons. "I was a clerk-typist with the army," remembers Newhart. "I was stationed in San Francisco. And actually if the North Koreans had overrun Hawaii, I would have been the guy who would have been between them and the rest of the country. I was the final defense of this land."

Next, he enrolled in law school at Loyola in the fall of 1954, but wound up flunking out in February of 1956. His mother, Pauline Newhart, said in a 1975 interview with *Good Housekeeping,* "He didn't hit the law books, so that flopped, and I suspect he thinks I wish he'd become an attorney. It's not true; I'm delighted with his career, but I never thought he'd end up in the entertainment field.

"But maybe we should have known, with his humor. When we used to watch movies on the late show, Bob's comments were funnier than the films."

After law school, Newhart was employed by a succession of different Chicago businesses over the course of the next four years. He worked as an accountant, an advertising copywriter, a bookkeeper, a clerk, and a shoe salesman, among other jobs. This experience in the nine-to-five workday world proved to be absolutely invaluable to Newhart, although at the time it must have seemed merely depressing. Many of his early monologues were closely based on what he did and what he saw during this period. He says, "I had a variety of jobs, full time and part time, which were very helpful for my comedy because I got to meet a lot of people."

Newhart describes himself as a good observer, and he remembers that he used to "jot down wryly caustic notes on the conversations and behavior of co-workers on their way to the office water cooler. . . . People aren't aware they're being imprinted for future use."

Back in those days he was an unassuming, almost painfully

shy young man. Newhart admits that he looked like "a guy you pass on the street every night and don't really notice." He says his features are "nondescript and colorless." Small wonder, then, that no one describes the young Bob Newhart as a Don Juan. In fact, he tended to be extremely nervous around women, especially the attractive ones, and his dates tended to be few and far between.

Dan Sorkin, a Chicago disk jockey who later gave a big boost to Newhart's career, recalls hearing that "Bob used to find himself riding in the elevator very often with this absolutely gorgeous girl who had a job on another floor of the same office building. He was just smitten, and he was trying to work up his courage to introduce himself and ask her for a date. But the problem was that there were usually lots of other people in the elevator. . . . One day, though, there was nobody else riding in the elevator, and she stepped in, and he was already there—so he finally had his big chance. Well, all the way down he kept screwing up his courage, but he couldn't manage to say anything. Just before the doors opened on the first floor, he tapped her on the shoulder. She turned around and smiled. And he stammered and said, 'Uh, did you know that my uncle's sick?' She just stared at him and walked away and that was the end of that."

At this point in his life Newhart considered himself to be, in his words, a "dismal failure." He remembers that he made up an elaborate fantasy about taking up the life of a forest ranger: "I'd be alone there in my little tower, and I'd read a lot of books I never got around to in college. I would play the jazz flute and piano. I wouldn't have to explain to anyone what I was doing. I'd be a black sheep to the family, and talked about in hushed tones at family reunions. 'Bob,' they'd say. 'We don't talk much about him. He, uh, he *plays the jazz flute and piano.*' Then, I thought, what if I got good at it? I'd have to go out and play for people. You have to let others know. Like writing a book—you don't burn it. That's probably why I'm in this business."

One job for which Newhart felt a considerable amount of antipathy was a position with an unemployment office. He says, "I once worked for the Illinois State Unemployment Compensation Board. I was behind the counter. Now the strange thing was that we who were working in the office got paid fifty-five dollars a week, while the people collecting unemployment, the claimants, got fifty. And they only had to come in one day a week. I put up with that for about two weeks, and then it suddenly dawned on me I was coming in four days a week for an extra five bucks."

The position that Newhart held for the longest amount of time during these years was that of accountant, mainly with the offices of U.S. Gypsum in Chicago. "I wasn't even a CPA, which requires passing a test," he explains. "I was more like a regular bookkeeper."

In his stand-up routines he often mentions his career as an accountant, saying that "my theory of accounting was that as long as you got within two or three bucks of it, you were all right. But that didn't catch on."

He soon realized he wasn't cut out for accounting when "at the end of the day I had to balance the petty cash with the slips—every time you give out money you had to get a slip. It had to balance. Well, I'd be there for three or four hours trying to figure out where the last dollar or dime went to. So finally I'd just take it out of my pocket and I'd put it in. If there were two dollars left over, I'd take it out. . . . And they told me you can't do that. You gotta find it. I said, 'You're paying me five dollars an hour to find two cents—it doesn't make sense.' So I wasn't a very good accountant."

Newhart says, "There are some days when I wish I were still sitting there with my green eyeshade and a garter on my sleeve. . . . Show business can get frantic, but on the whole I would say that my demise as an accountant was mutually beneficial to all concerned."

"Newhart was an accountant in the engineering department at U.S. Gypsum around '56 and '57," remembers Carl Flaws, a former employee of the company. Flaws says Newhart wasn't really as poor an accountant as he has said in his monologues: "I think that was all exaggeration for the comedy, joking about what he had to do." Another former U.S. Gypsum employee, Allen Drachman, says that "Newhart was no world-beater, but I believe he did his job well. People liked him."

In the opinion of Jack Spatafora, Newhart had no clear plan at this time about what he wanted to do in the future. "I don't know if Bob ever made a firm decision to pursue his show-business career rather than the accounting, to sacrifice everything for success as an entertainer. I think his idea was just to do both, and see which one worked out better for him."

In the late fifties Newhart was occasionally appearing with several small amateur theatrical groups. Joe Coan, who was then a member of The Edmund Players, says that "I remember him as a shy guy who used to come around to be in our plays. Nobody paid that much attention to him. He'd help with the scenery and do little bit parts in productions. . . . He was just another guy to most of the other actors; he stayed in the background, mostly."

Newhart recalls, "I did a play, long time ago, called *The Golden Fleecing*. Talk about bombing! The play was awful and I was awful. It was in Hillside, the tent theater, and we were on the glide path to the airport and there was a slight incline on the expressway there. Between the trucks going back into second gear and the planes landing, it was a mess. The theater isn't there anymore, and I feel I may have had something to do with that."

Says Mariette Le Blanc, "I went out to one of those tent theater shows. Now in those days there were all kinds of tent theaters around Chicago. These were plays put on by small companies, where they would pitch a huge tent—and inside it would be the audience, where they would watch the play, usually 'in the round.' I remember that Bob once asked me how he had done in the play, and I replied, as politely as I could, that he was improving.

"What I liked about him was that he was willing to work at it. He didn't have a big head. He was willing to get involved in stage plays so that he could understand how that medium worked. . . . He studied all the facets of his art. By the time he was ready to do *The Button-Down Mind* and eventually his television shows, he had already done his homework."

As he was nearing his thirtieth birthday, though, Newhart was still concerned about whether or not he would ever really become successful at anything. Spatafora recalls that "Bob was probably feeling very frustrated because a lot of his peers were already moving on ahead, while his life seemed to be going in circles; he was drifting along, dreaming of a show-business career. And that situation continued for several years.

"By the late fifties Bob had started to slip away from many of the members of our group. Part of the reason I think for that was because he felt as if he had been left behind by some of his more prosperous friends who had gotten married and started having families, buying homes, and so forth. . . . Of course, the supreme irony was that it was Bob who—lo and behold—came out of hiding and eventually achieved much, much greater acclaim than anybody else."

As a relief from some of the tedium at one of his office jobs, Newhart and a friend, Ed Gallagher, would entertain themselves by trying to make each other laugh over the telephone. (Gallagher, who was then an advertising copywriter for the Leo Burnett Company in Chicago, and Newhart had first met when they worked together on a production with a small theatrical group.) Newhart remembers that they would dream up some highly unusual situations. He might, for instance, call Ed one afternoon and say to him, in a disguised voice, "You don't know me, Mr. Gallagher, but I'm a United Airlines pilot. I just picked your name out of the telephone book. We took off from Midway Airport half an hour ago, but the co-pilot and I got to horsing around in the cabin, and we both fell out. The plane is still up there with fifty-seven people on board. I tried to call Midway and tell them about it, but they just hang up on me and say, 'Why don't you leave us alone?' I thought you might call them and explain things."

Gallagher's response to this might then be to ask Newhart, "How'd you say you happened to fall out of the plane, Captain?" The two of them would play along with this craziness for as long as they could continue to think of something amusing to say.

Eventually, they hit on the idea of taping some of these

conversations and trying to sell them to radio stations. They felt this might be a way of getting into show business. Newhart explains that these conversations were the genesis of his comedy routines: "The bit . . . about the submarine commander addressing his crew ("The Cruise of the U.S.S. Codfish") grew out of the tapes Gallagher and I did. Ed pretended to be a radio announcer. Then he'd throw me any situation that popped into his head. Out of nowhere he came up with, 'This is Ed Gallagher. We're taking you to the U.S.S. Codfish, which is about to surface in New York harbor. We're going to talk to the commander of the Codfish. . . . Take it away, commander.' Then Ed would duck down the hall to work our tape machine, leaving me with the situation. I've never been on a submarine, but as the commander of the submarine Codfish, I ad-libbed a speech to the crew for fifteen or twenty minutes. That original routine was terrible, but when we edited it, it was pretty good."

So in early 1959 they began sending out some of these tapes to about one hundred radio stations around the country. They found a man on the West Coast who said he could get ten stations out there to buy their routines. Newhart and Gallagher then decided to charge ten dollars per station per week: this would add up to a total of one hundred dollars a week they would be paid for doing five different five-minute comedy routines. Besides these ten stations they had originally lined up, they also soon managed to locate three others on their own and sign contracts with them. This made thirteen stations altogether, and it looked as though the scheme was working out pretty well.

But then they were hit with some disappointing news—the

West Coast stations were no longer interested. "They were owned by one man," Newhart says. "And on second thought he felt that our stuff was too sophisticated for his audience. There we were, stuck with only three customers. After Ed and I had sent those stations tapes for thirteen weeks, we were . . . in the red."

Newhart recalls that the three stations to air the tapes were located in Jacksonville, Florida; Idaho Falls, Idaho; and Northhampton, Massachusetts. "And then one of the three stations stiffed us, wouldn't pay anything," he says. "Now the two other stations wanted to renew us after thirteen weeks, but we had to write them back and say we couldn't afford to do the program anymore. It cost us forty dollars a week in tapes alone."

Jack Spatafora says, "I thought those tapes that Ed Gallagher and Bob made were very funny. They were sort of inspired by the comedy of Bob and Ray. . . . At first nobody was buying the tapes, but in trying to sell them Gallagher and Bob connected up with Dan Sorkin, who was a popular radio announcer and deejay in Chicago at the time. Dan didn't use the tapes, but he said to Bob, 'I think I could use you as comedy relief of a kind on a show I'm developing.'"

"Ed Gallagher played me one of those tapes," remembers Sorkin, "and I immediately thought that Bob was one of the freshest, most creative comedians I had heard in years. He seemed to fit right in there on the same level with people like Nichols and May, Shelley Berman, and Jonathan Winters.

"Those tapes were mainly Newhart's routines: Ed would tend to be more of a straight man on them. . . . Bob's stuff was already incredible. Some of the bits were already very polished. His delivery was excellent and he had exquisite timing. He made it all seem so easy—sort of like Frank Sinatra's singing, where it sounds like anyone could do it but then if *you* try to do it, you find it's not really so easy after all. I think Bob's stuff is universal. It's just as funny today as it was then. He had a real common touch: everyone can identify with the things he talks about."

Newhart became a regular on Sorkin's program on WCFL radio in Chicago. Spatafora remembers that "the first time Bob was on one of Dan's shows he played a guy in the audience who kept interrupting the host."

"Bob was on my program many times," says Sorkin. "Whatever was in the news at the time, I would interview Bob as an expert on the subject. If the stock market was on the way down, he would be an analyst. If there had been a major fire in Chicago, he was the owner of the building. If there was a scandal in the state administration, then he was the controller. Everything that Bob said was made up on the spot. Nothing was written down or planned on the show. Bob was marvelous at ad-libbing."

"In addition to my radio show I also briefly had a TV show," Sorkin recalls. "It was a live variety show and it ran for two weeks. Bob was the only good thing on it—I was okay on the radio but just terrible on television. This show was done for the NBC TV station in Chicago."

Newhart and Sorkin quickly became friends. Sorkin says Newhart was just as funny off the air as he was when he was performing. "Bob was one of those guys who just *thinks* funny. It didn't matter whether he was writing a routine or you were just talking to him—it was the same dry sense of humor. . . .

Bob is a rarity. He is painfully honest, very shy, and incredibly talented. Bob is introverted, but somehow he also loves to perform. He is generous to a fault. He's sensitive, intelligent. Deeply religious. He took care of his parents very well after he became successful. Everybody seemed to get along well with Bob."

Sorkin played a pivotal role in Newhart's career; in fact, if anyone could be said to have "discovered" Newhart, Sorkin would be that man. Besides the exposure he was giving Newhart on the radio, Sorkin was telling everyone he met about this bright young comedian. One especially important move was when Sorkin brought him to the attention of Frank Hogan, who became Newhart's personal manager.

Meanwhile, Newhart was still forced to work at a variety of other jobs in order to make ends meet. Remembers Sorkin, "One of Bob's jobs around that time was at Abercrombie and Fitch, which was an elite department store in Chicago. Bob was a salesman on the floor there, but I guess he didn't last too long. When somebody asked him how much, say, a pair of binoculars cost, Bob might reply, 'Fifty dollars.' Then if the customer said, 'That's too much,' Bob might say, 'Well, how about forty-five?'

"At another time I tried to get him a job as a disk jockey at a small station in Michigan—I think it was in Battle Creek. But Bob was nervous, he didn't do too well at the audition. I told the station manager he was crazy not to hire him. Looking back on it, however, it's a good thing Bob didn't get that job, or he might have been stuck there for too long."

Newhart's next important job as a comedian was at another Chicago TV station. He was hired by Red Quinlain, who recalls that "Bob worked for me at channel 7, the ABC affiliate in Chicago—the call letters then were WBKB. I was the vice president in charge of the station, and I tried him out in several different formats. None of them were all that popular, but that wasn't Bob's fault. We just didn't quite know how to do justice to him. The problem was that he had a few monologues already, and they were terrific, but they only lasted four or five minutes. After he gave one of them, what else could he do to fill the rest of a thirty-minute show? Plus, we didn't have much money to spend on production.

"So I had him on a man-in-the-street interview show. It was broadcast in the mornings and lasted about five weeks. Bob would stand on the corner and he would talk to the people who came by. This was all done live; we strung a cable from our twelfth-floor studios down to where he was on the street. It was always comedy; this wasn't a serious-discussion type of thing. Sort of like David Letterman does now."

Quinlain explains he had some unusual problems in finding the money to pay Newhart. "I had Bob on my musicians' payroll," he says, "because I didn't have any other way to budget it. We had a really tough contract with the local musicians' union. We had a quota to hire forty musicians, but we didn't need anywhere near that number. . . . However, the union was very lax as far as who they would give a card to. So Bob went over there and hit some bongo drums once or twice, paid his money, and he was in."

"I wanted to help him get ahead," says Quinlain. "I liked him, and it was clear he was very promising. I figured it was just a matter of time before he'd be saying good-bye to me and going on to bigger and better things. And that's exactly what happened. He was only at the station for a few months."

In 1959 Newhart was finding his style as a comedian. His humor was dry and cerebral, and fit right in with the current trend in comics—he had much in common with people such as Mort Sahl and Shelley Berman. But those who knew Newhart then say he wasn't consciously attempting to follow any particular trend. He was simply doing what was natural for him, what he thought was funny.

Just as Newhart himself was soft-spoken, the comedy routines that he was developing were never heavy-handed. He talked to listeners in the civil tones of ordinary conversation, and assumed they would have the discernment to understand him. And Newhart was in no hurry when he delivered his monologues to go quickly for the easy laugh or the snappy punch lines. He might spend a few minutes setting up a situation that would only pay off at the end. He invited audiences to listen to what he had to say, hoping they would happen to agree that it was funny. He was never one to come out, as Milton Berle did, in drag or in a clown's suit, announcing from the beginning that he was supposed to be hilarious. (Often, the comedian who proclaims, with a merry twinkle, that he is going to make us roll in the aisles actually produces the opposite of the intended effect: we determinedly clinch our teeth and grimly defy him to get so much as a chuckle past our lips.)

Newhart explains that many other humorists had a significant effect on him. "I was always interested in comedy, and admittedly influenced by Bob and Ray, Bob Benchley, Jack Benny, Dick Van Dyke, and even George Bernard Shaw. To me, comedy was looking at life obliquely. I knew I made people laugh but I was never sure why. But slowly my confidence began to build. That's really what it's all about, a series of confidence-building steps until one day you're the star of your own show."

Jack Spatafora says, "Bob told me once that he saw life with a certain kind of warp, and that when he recounted what he saw, it was funny."

Not everybody recognized Newhart's talents as quickly as Sorkin, Hogan, and Quinlain had. Spatafora remembers one of the first evenings on which Newhart tried out his routines. "Before Bob did his first record he wasn't big enough to get into the important nightclubs. He tried out bits and pieces of some of his monologues at parties and on those tapes with Ed Gallagher. . . . He also tried out some of his early stuff at local amateur performances, like at some of the local churches. I recall going to one of those performances at a church, and Bob did some funny, funny stuff—but it was all in Bob's usual droll, straight-faced style. I remember the audience just sort of sat on their hands because they didn't quite understand it. They were waiting for balloons to burst or pratfalls to happen. And Bob just didn't do those things. He was a little ahead of the local Chicago market."

3

THE
BUTTON-DOWN
MIND

At this point Newhart and Ed Gallagher must have felt that their plan to sell their comic routines to radio stations had turned out to be a flop: after all, they wound up losing $350 on the deal. Soon afterward, Gallagher took a job with an advertising firm in New York, leaving Newhart to pursue his career as a solo comedy act in Chicago. Newhart was occasionally getting spots on local radio and television stations, but those jobs paid very little and Newhart still believed he would probably have to spend at least a few more years working as an accountant, adding up countless more columns of figures, or at some other equally dull office job. He was still feeling more than a little dissatisfied with the way things were going.

But his big break came very soon, and changed his life completely. In November 1959, Dan Sorkin, the disk jockey at WCFL, helped to introduce Newhart to executives from Warner Brothers Records. James Conkling, then the president of Warner Brothers Records, and Hal Cook, then Warner's vice president in charge of sales, were visiting Chicago at the time, and Newhart played them tapes of three of his monologues. Conkling and Cook were both immediately enthusiastic about what they heard.

Conkling remembers, "Warner's had a distributor in Chicago who got the tapes from Dan Sorkin and told us Newhart was great—that he had some of the funniest stuff you've ever heard—and that we *had* to listen to his routines. . . . Actually, we came sort of under protest; we had a plane to catch. We didn't have any idea how good he would turn out to be. At any rate, I and Hal Cook and a few other people, we had a couple of free hours, and the Warner's distributor's place was close to the airport. We got there that afternoon, and Bob was waiting for us. I learned later that he had come by bus or trolley because he didn't have enough money for a car.

"It was at the far end of the warehouse, and it was sort of dark. There were no chairs or tables around. It was the place where records were piled up to be sent to the factory. Bob was pale, congenial, and quiet—not cracking jokes at all. Seemed quite serious. Then he turned on the machine and played us his tapes. He didn't laugh at his own stuff, but we did. The first one was the Abraham Lincoln routine, and it absolutely floored us. . . . There were a couple of other very funny ones, too. And we said to ourselves right away that it would be ridiculous not to record him. At the time, about the only comedian on records was Shelley Berman, who was doing quite well. And here we were a new company looking for unique artists. We immediately thought this could be a tremendous hit.

"I've auditioned thousands of singers and other performers, but I've never had anything else happen the way it did with

Bob. I have never ever been so sure of something. He didn't even have to finish the Abraham Lincoln thing for it to be clear. He was an original, a real talent. It was so refreshing. Usually you have to go see the artist three or four times, talk it over with other people—and then you're usually still not sure about them. Not so with Bob."

A week later, Newhart's monologues were heard by George Avakian, who was then Warner's director of artists and repertory. "The astonishing thing," recalls Avakian, "was that the routines were already very polished and well developed. And his delivery was fine. He didn't have to make many changes at all. He was more than good enough to record."

Avakian remembers saying, "Bob, this is very good, but the one thing I'd like to recommend is that it will be even more effective and more commercial if we record you live in front of an audience during one of your engagements, because then we'll get the reaction of the audience, the applause and laughter and so on. It'll add an extra dimension. And I believe that this'll be the first live comedy record album ever made."

About his meeting with the Warner Brothers executives, Newhart recalls that "they were somewhat impressed, and they said, 'We'd like to record your next nightclub performance.' And I said, 'I've never played a nightclub.'" So, Newhart explains, the next step was for them to find the right place in which he could perform his monologues. He says they wanted to avoid recording in Chicago, where Newhart's friends might pack the audience and laugh too loudly at everything he said. Instead, they selected a club in Houston called The Tidelands.

According to Conkling, "We had a big problem finding

where he could perform, mainly because he was unknown. None of the clubs in Chicago would take him."

Avakian says, "I played Bob's tape for the managers of some of the nightclubs in New York. And everybody said, 'That sounds good, but it's not for us.' They also said, 'It's a little strange. Who's interested in a guy pretending he's talking on the telephone?' Of course, when the album became a smash those same people were clamoring to get him to come to their clubs."

After several weeks of searching to find a place, Frank Hogan, who was then Newhart's manager, found the club in Houston. "But the audience at The Tidelands was really small," remembers Conkling. "If you listen to the first Newhart LP carefully, you can tell there weren't many people there."

"I was terrified of playing in front of this audience," says Newhart. "But I went out there with my three original routines, plus a few more I'd written in the meantime, and I looked straight ahead and did them. They went over very well and when I came offstage after taking my bow, the club manager said, 'They want more. Go back and give 'em an encore.' And I said, 'But I don't have any more material.'

"So I went back out there and thanked the crowd. And then I said, 'Now which one of those routines would you like to hear again?'"

"We taped Bob on two evenings at The Tidelands," says Avakian. "Bob was a little more nervous the first night. The second night, basically, is where most of the material on that first album comes from. . . . Sometimes I took some of one night's performance and combined it with the other night's performance of the same routine. One track on the record would contain elements from both nights' shows. Also, he didn't do the routines in exactly the same way. They were pretty much set, but he would still improvise a few things: he might give a particular line a different kind of reading.

"Bob was really scared and nervous about the whole thing. He felt he hadn't done such a great job, but I reassured him that it was fine. . . . What I especially liked was that he's got this deadpan delivery where he seems so serious and doesn't seem to realize that what he's saying is a little goofy. Bob has this wonderfully naïve quality to his voice. He sounds very earnest. His character seems baffled at why everyone is laughing at him."

Newhart's performance at The Tidelands was recorded in February 1960, *The Button-Down Mind of Bob Newhart* was released in April, and by summer it had reached the number-one spot on the LP charts. It became the first comedy recording to sell over one million copies; Newhart was, in fact, the first comic to become famous because of a record. Soon he was appearing regularly on television variety programs such as "The Ed Sullivan Show," "The Garry Moore Show," and "The Jack Paar Show." He had become a celebrity in a matter of a few months.

Says Conkling, "Some of the New York sales people for Warner's were skeptical at first, they thought the record would never sell. They told us not to put it out. . . . But it was a smash, an overnight success like none I've ever seen. We couldn't press the records fast enough."

Conkling recalls that Newhart was surprised at his own success. "He was modest and shy, but I think he knew he was funny. He probably thought, 'Some sharp guys may pick up on my stuff, but it'll probably never have a big audience.'"

"At Warner's we had a very good promotional staff," Conkling explains, "and they were tied in very closely with our distributors, who were in charge of getting records into the local stores. Several of our promotional people were very high on Bob Newhart, and they were flooding distributors with material about him. . . . And the distributors often had good relations with the deejays.

"I think 'The Driving Instructor' was the first track on the album that was played on the radio. 'The Driving Instructor' was broken on a San Francisco radio station, and they got a very good response to it from listeners. That's one of the things that got the ball rolling for Bob."

Jack Spatafora credits the shrewdness of Frank Hogan for some of the rapidness of Newhart's rise to fame. Says Spatafora, "Of course it was a combination of a lot of things. That record was really funny, and the time must have been just right for this kind of a thing. But I think you'd also have to say that another reason was that 'Tweet' Hogan [Tweet was Frank Hogan's nickname] was very smart about getting the album talked about. There were an awful lot of things dropped in the newspapers about Bob. I remember one thing in particular: Bing Crosby was doing a movie at that time, and Tweet made sure he sent a copy of the album to Crosby. He felt Crosby would get a kick out of it—and he did. And so the story went around to several of the columnists that during breaks from the shooting over at Paramount, Bing Crosby and the rest of the cast were playing this record of Bob Newhart's. So it was a great way of name-dropping. Tweet did a lot of things of that kind.

"Eventually, it became a sort of an inside thing—that there was a very different kind of a comedian performing in a very different kind of a way, on a record instead of a nightclub, and you could get him for $3.98. And the story started spreading in that fashion.

"Then disk jockeys began playing examples of it, and therein was a way of promoting comedy that wasn't available to other comics who you'd have to see to be able to appreciate. A deejay could play a cut from Newhart's album and suddenly maybe 100,000 people in the city had all heard it at once. It would take years for such a number of people to have actually been exposed to a comedian in person. The record cut through all that. . . . He made a quantum leap with the album. In a matter of a very few years, with very little pain and suffering, he became a big star. He didn't have to grind it out like a lot of the other comedians, like a George Burns or a Jack Benny, who would talk about working their way up from the Lower East Side of New York, spending years on the circuit in the Catskills, and so forth. Bob never had to do that. He went from oblivion to celebrity. . . . It was a whole different way of going up the ladder of success."

The Button-Down Mind of Bob Newhart received unanimous approval in the press. Every review was glowingly favorable. For instance, the critic from *Hi-Fi/Stereo Review* wrote, "I had never heard Bob Newhart before receiving this record. I am sure we shall all hear a great deal of him from now on. For Mr. Newhart is certainly one of the funniest, most original of the modern group of comics who are not afraid to use the night-club stage as a platform from which to make observations about the world in which we live."

In *The New York Times,* Gilbert Millstein said that "what he does is heavily satirical of sacred cows, so that the total New-hart can infuse a scarifying assault on the body politic with the ruddy glow of health or bite the hand feeding him and make it feel like a manicure."

"Thirty-one-year-old Bob Newhart . . . represents the over-night influx of a whole new tribe of comics who are really satirists," said Pete Martin, writing for the *Saturday Evening Post*. "They comment with devastating irreverence on anything and everything, old and new, current or historical. Nothing is sacrosanct to them. Their humor is far more cerebral than evis-ceral, but they fetch just as many laughs as the [Phil] Silvers school."

Part of the reason for Newhart's almost overnight rise to stardom was that he had created a unique style that audiences could easily recognize. People could hear at once that he was different from other comedians. As Newhart explains, "I was at the right place at the right time. Prior to then, guys would do 'Take my wife, please' or 'My wife is so mean . . .' and *anybody* could steal that. Then it changed. Guys had to come up with their own material. You couldn't steal Shelley Ber-man, because people would say, 'That sounds like Shelley Ber-man.' They couldn't steal my stuff, either, because anyone would have been able to identify it as sounding 'just like Bob Newhart.'" Instead of a string of one-liners, he would develop a little story in his monologues. The laughs would come out of the situation and the characters: if you quoted one of his lines, it wouldn't be funny when taken out of context. (Strangely enough, this trend in stand-up comedy has reversed itself, and many of today's young comics, like Steven Wright, are doing one-liners again.)

"In the monologues when I first started," Newhart says, "it was mainly these insane comments coming out of a straight face. That's what made the comedy. An example would be my routine ["The Cruise of the U.S.S. Codfish"] on the submarine commander who has just come out of this horrendous trip, and is handling it very calmly. He's telling his crew: 'I've got some very good news. We just broke the record for surfacing, firing at a target, and then resubmerging. We took four minutes and twenty-nine seconds off the previous record, and I want to congratulate all you men on the precision you displayed. At the same time, I don't in any way mean to slight the contribution made by the men we had to leave on deck.'"

Newhart's style of delivery was an essential part of his humor. He spoke in a diffident way; he sounded hesitant, almost apologetic—like one of those nonentities who are so unimpressive that they feel they have to reintroduce themselves to us every time we meet them. Newhart used this disarmingly mild-mannered way of talking as a vehicle for delivering his sharp satiric thrusts.

So adept was he at using this technique, that the kinds of people he was ridiculing were probably unaware of what was being done to them—they laughed right along with the rest of us.

Often, Newhart would portray characters who gradually gave themselves away as being avaricious, status-seeking phonies and hypocrites. But this was always revealed in a subtle way, never blatantly or in such a manner that it was clear that a heavy-handed Statement was being made. For that reason, Newhart was able to achieve a level of popularity that comedians such as Lenny Bruce could never reach. While Bruce obviously had an anti-Establishment message to deliver, you had to listen carefully to detect Newhart's anger at what was happening in America. (If Lenny Bruce sometimes came on like an angry prophet, Bob Newhart usually appeared to be like the guy who meekly asks if it's okay to come in and check the meter.)

His comedy usually had to do with his revolt against the monotony of the life of the average guy. Newhart's point of view was that large organizations and modern technology were threatening to stamp out all traces of natural, spontaneous feelings. As Newhart explains, "I have a pet peeve [that] runs through my humor—the impersonal corporate bigness in modern life, and the individual getting lost."

Even though he became popular in the sixties, Newhart's humor is clearly rooted in the fifties: he deals with the edgy anxieties of that era when Americans were building atomic bomb shelters in their backyards and reading books such as *The Hidden Persuaders, The Organization Man,* and *The Lonely Crowd.* It's probably no coincidence that when social protests became more unrestrained in the late sixties, Newhart's stand-up routines seemed to fall out of favor with the public.

When asked to explain what the phrase "button-down mind" means, Newhart replies, "To me, they're kind of ink-blot-test words—whatever they mean to you, that's what they mean. Since some of my routines have to do with advertising, and since the button-down collar seems to be part of the uniform worn on Madison Avenue, the words 'button-down mind' have a Madison Avenue flavor to me."

Newhart describes his routines as "based on circumstances and conversations which might happen if you carry things a little farther than they go in real life." He also says that he prides himself on being a careful observer of people and that much of his comedy is derived from what he has seen around him, especially during those years in the fifties when he worked for many different businesses.

There's no question that Newhart is a good listener, for his comedy monologues show that he has a sharp ear for the vernacular. He often catches the exact turns of phrase that make us recognize the speaker as an ordinary American—the night watchman, the bus driver, or the accountant. His best routines are also very tightly written, with nearly every word contributing to the humor and with nothing superfluous. If Newhart ever wanted to, he probably could write some excellent short stories, just as other fine comedians, such as Woody Allen, have done. Newhart feels, though, that his goal as a writer is to create something that can be performed, not just words on a page. Publishers have frequently approached him about writing a book, but he has always turned them down. (When he was first told about this biography for St. Martin's Press, he replied, "Why would anybody want to do a book about me? It would have to be about eight pages long.")

In his monologues Newhart's characters tend to stammer quite a lot, and often don't speak in complete sentences—just like people out of real life. Newhart explains that he does this deliberately. "People don't finish sentences," he says. "They slur their words, and so on. I can't imagine a worse situation for me than spending an evening with someone like Noel Coward. No one's that brilliant or sophisticated or chi-chi or able to finish a sentence down to the last polished word. I'd get exhausted trying to keep up."

The Button-Down Mind of Bob Newhart contains some of his best-written and most effective routines. The first track on the LP, "Abe Lincoln Versus Madison Avenue," is a comic gem, and it's also Newhart's most famous routine. In this bit, he plays a PR man advising President Lincoln on how to create the right public image.

On stage, Newhart introduced the routine by explaining how the idea suggested itself to him. "Many of you may have read *The Hidden Persuaders*," Newhart said to the audience. "One of the points the book made was that the real danger of the public relations man or the advertising man was that they were creating images. And the author felt that in the presidential campaigns the candidates were getting closer and closer together, so that there was no real difference between them, and you were really voting for the personality. And this got me to thinking: supposing this science were as far advanced during the Civil War as it is today—and there was no Lincoln. Now the advertising people, realizing this, would have had to create a Lincoln. And I think they would have gone about it something like this. This is a telephone conversation between Abe and his press agent, just before Gettysburg."

The press agent is appalled that "Lincoln" is thinking of shaving off his beard. He reminds the President (who doesn't seem to be terribly bright) that the beard, the stovepipe hat, and the shawl all contribute to his "image." The PR man is careful not to get too angry with Lincoln, though, since he doesn't want to lose one of his most important clients. He's very understanding, and he explains the situation to Abe patiently, almost as if he were addressing a slow-witted schoolboy. When Lincoln tells him he's planning on changing "four score and seven" to "eighty-seven," the PR man says, "I understand it means the same thing, Abe . . . but it would sort of be like Marc Antony saying, 'Friends, Romans, and countrymen—I've got somethin' I wanna tell ya.' You see what I mean?"

And then Abe has another complaint: "What else? . . . 'People will little note nor long remember' . . . Abe, what could possibly be wrong with that? . . . They'll remember it . . . Abe, of course they'll remember it. It's the old humble bit. You can't say, 'It's a great speech, I think everybody's gonna remember it.' You come off a braggart, don't you see that? . . . Abe, will ya just give the speech the way Charlie wrote it?"

Near the end of the conversation the press agent tells Lincoln to grab a pencil and write down this quotation: "You can fool all of the people some of the time and some of the people all of the time, but you can't fool all the people all the time." Apparently, Abe has been getting this mixed up, and he's been telling reporters, "You can fool all the people all the time."

Newhart delivers the monologues on the *Button-Down Mind* LP in his characteristic manner: The man he is portraying usually gives a speech or holds a telephone conversation, but we only hear one side of it. And Newhart pauses throughout, indicating those times when the other person is supposed to be speaking. Because Newhart does such a convincing job of delivering his words, we feel that we can clearly imagine everything that's being said by the other characters.

The Button-Down Mind of Bob Newhart includes several other choice monologues besides "Abe Lincoln," such as the speech of the captain of a nuclear submarine ("The Cruise of the U.S.S. Codfish") to his men just as they're about to end a voyage that has lasted two years. He admits that "our firing on Miami Beach can best be termed 'ill-timed.'" But he feels that "because it happened on what they call in the newspaper business a 'a slow news day,' it received a lot more space than I think it deserved—since it was the off-season down there."

In "Merchandizing the Wright Brothers," a promoter talks to Orville Wright about the commercial potentialities for the airplane. Not surprisingly, the businessman is disturbed to hear the inventor say that the passengers would have to lie on the wings. Even worse, "You only went a hundred and five feet, huh? . . . That's all? . . . And the twelve guys still had to push it down the hill? . . . Gee, that's gonna cut our time down to the coast."

Another monologue ("The Khrushchev Landing Rehearsal") is about the arrival of Premier Khrushchev in Washington. Newhart imagines that TV producers are staging the whole thing for the maximum impact before the cameras. At one point a frustrated producer barks out, "All right, all right . . . Somebody take him over to Ike. . . . Introduce him to Ike. . . . That's it . . . now somebody take the putter away from Ike."

"Nobody Will Ever Play Baseball" is an imaginary conversation between Abner Doubleday and a game manufacturer, played by Newhart. Newhart's character has a great deal of trouble making sense of the rules for baseball. "Yes . . . Yes . . . Three strikes and you're out," says the game manufacturer. "Yes . . . Yes . . . and three balls . . . oh, four balls . . . Why *four* balls, Mr. Doubleday? . . . You mean nobody ever asked you before?"

One of the cleverest routines on the album is "The Driving Instructor." It's a good example of the way that Newhart likes to "carry things a little farther than they go in real life." This bit, according to Newhart, is dedicated to "a group of men who every day go to work and never know for sure if they'll return that night, because they face death in a hundred different ways. I'm talking about America's driving instructors." Newhart portrays an instructor who gets into a car with an extremely dangerous woman driver. He learns that she has had one previous lesson, and he asks her about it: "Who was the instructor on that, Mrs. Webb? . . . Mr. Adams? . . . Just let me read ahead here and kind of familiarize myself with the case . . . Um, just how fast were you going when Mr. Adams jumped from the car? . . . Seventy-five? . . . And where was that? . . . In your *driveway*? . . . How far had Mr. Adams gotten in the lesson? . . . Backing out?"

Jack Spatafora remembers that when the *Button-Down Mind* LP was released, Newhart told him, "When we cut that album, it was a very exciting evening—but I don't know where it'll go from here. My problem is that if it goes anywhere big I'm in trouble because I exhausted my entire repertoire that night. I'm afraid I'd really have to scramble fast to produce enough material to fill another record."

Newhart's fears proved to be well founded. (Although, it must be admitted, he was encountering a problem that most comedians would love to be faced with.) Throughout 1960 Newhart worked especially hard at his writing. When he wasn't performing one of his old routines, he was usually trying to polish a new one. His standards were very high, and he wound up discarding most of what he wrote. He didn't want to put anything on his next album that would be just filler.

He wanted it all to be good. There were many routines he performed a few times that year in nightclubs, but which he never recorded or did on television.

"That, I suppose, is what I love to do—or hate to do—most. Write," Newhart says. "If the stuff flows, you're in heaven. If it doesn't, you're in hell." This comment on writing seems quite revealing. While Newhart has continued to write stand-up monologues throughout his career—and has continued to come up with amusing material—he has done much less writing in recent years. What's more, he has often worked with collaborators on his more recent routines. The pressures he must have faced early in his career to produce large quantities of humorous material must have been enormous, and he clearly prefers to write at a slower pace today.

Newhart explains that when he's working on a new routine, he writes down a few ideas and then makes a tape recording to see how it sounds. "At first I don't write all of it down, just four or five of the points I want to make. Then I use them as going-off points. I might spend two hours working out a routine, as I did with my Lincoln bit, or I might spend ten hours on a routine and be hung up and have to walk away from it because it's not going anywhere. I've spent as much as a month on one monologue, playing tapes back to myself and enlarging upon them."

As Newhart writes, he worries about making his comedy overly difficult for audiences to follow. "If I'm too subtle I defeat my purpose. I lay a bomb," he says. "Who knows where the line lies between not hitting my listeners over the head with a meat ax and nobody understanding what I'm talking about? I have to grope for it."

"I like to lay into foibles, affectations, pretensions," explains Newhart. "I shy away from politics, not because it is perishable but for another reason. The subjects I like to needle need jabbing regardless of politics."

And he tends to avoid putting any explicit "messages" into his comedy, even though he does have a very definite point of view on many issues. "Some comedians," he said in an interview in 1961, "like Mort Sahl and Lenny Bruce, can take off on a social evil and work from there. I just can't do it. I don't know how. For me, the idea has to be funny first. If it builds up to knock down a few straw men, then fine.

"I'll give you an example. One of the things that really boils me these days is the way young kids go out hunting for jobs. They're not interested in the kind of work or whether they'll be happy at it." (This sounds like a topic that would be even more relevant in the eighties than it was in the early sixties.) "They just want to know: How big a pension does the company offer?

"Think of that. They haven't got their first job yet. But already they're looking forward to retiring and living off a monthly paycheck.

"Now, to me, that's ripe material for a good sketch. But I just can't make it jell. And the reason is I started with a message instead of a funny idea. Weird, huh?"

When asked if the names of the characters he portrays in his monologues are all fictitious, he replies, "Well, the names aren't supposed to be those of real people. But even there a guy can't be sure. On a TV show in Chicago once, I made up a name—Telfer Mook. Now would you think parents with the name of Mook would name a child Telfer? [But] it happened. The fellow lives just outside Chicago, and he complained."

Suddenly, with the success of his first album, Newhart's whole way of life had become very different. Here he had been an unassuming, cola-drinking, church-going young accountant, just a face in the crowd, and now big-time Hollywood agents were courting his favors. Newspaper columnists were trying to figure out how to label him. His salary jumped from $200 to $5,000 a week. It was almost enough to make his head spin.

"Everything happened too quickly," Newhart says. "Every month it was something new. I was on 'The Garry Moore Show.' I was on 'The Ed Sullivan Show.' If I turned or shut my eyes for a moment, my salary soared."

He told an interviewer for the *Saturday Evening Post* in 1961 that "I know it's off the cob, but at times it seems . . . that what's going on is not really happening to me, but to a stranger. This is especially true when I watch myself on television. If I think about it for a moment, I really know I'm the person up there on that screen, but that message doesn't register automatically with me."

Newhart says he has always had the irrational fear that "one day some guy will walk up to me and tap me on the shoulder and say, 'Sorry, Bob, but it's all been a big mistake—you've got to return all the money and go back to being an accountant.' "

Yet in spite of all of his strange new experiences and feelings, Newhart managed to handle his newfound status very well. He didn't allow becoming a celebrity to change his level-headed approach to life. Perhaps this was due to his solid upbringing. Or because he didn't become famous until he was over thirty and mature enough to deal with success. At any rate, he never became another burned-out remnant of the sixties the way so many other entertainers did.

In October 1960 a reporter for the *New York Herald Tribune* asked him if he could manage the new pressures on him. "I can handle it all right," Newhart replied. "It's hard work and some people don't realize it. A guy asked me the other day how much I was earning, and I told him. Then he asked me how many minutes I perform each night, and I told him. And he said, 'You get a lot of money!'

"And I said, 'It may be only two and a half hours of performance before an audience each night, but it's equal to eight hours' work in some other job.' Besides, I've got to put in another eight hours a day preparing the act, seeing people, being interviewed, et cetera. . . . Most of the time, now, I'm very tired."

As a matter of fact, his performing schedule was so demanding that he recalls he would "sometimes long for the old in-and-out baskets" at U.S. Gypsum. "There's a certain satisfaction at the end of the day of having transferred a pile of papers from one side of the desk to the other. In comedy, the papers stay in one place for days."

He says that when he was an accountant he had plenty of free time but no money, and he had a lot of trouble getting dates. After his record came out, he found that he had plenty of money but no free time.

Although Newhart was then appearing regularly at nightclubs such as the hungry i in San Francisco, he was never all that fond of them: "It's the drunks. My act depends on illusion—I create scenes in the imagination—and every time I have to step out of a scene to put one of these birds in his place it kills the routine." He soon learned that his act went over more effectively in concert halls and college auditoriums.

His TV guest appearances also went well, since the television audiences were attentive and sober. "Those early TV guest shots on 'The Tonight Show' and all the variety shows were paradise," he remembers.

It's fascinating to look today at kinescopes of his early appearances on programs such as "The Ed Sullivan Show." (The Museum of Broadcasting in New York has several of them in its archives.) Newhart looks like a very callow young man, more like a guy in his twenties than a man in his thirties—the only jarring note is his hairline, which has already receded to a point near where it is today. Usually Newhart looks fairly nervous on these broadcasts. He often doesn't seem to know what to do with his hands. The viewer can imagine that if one were standing next to him, it might be apparent that he was trembling. What's more, he seems a bit too eager to get off the stage after his act is over. (Within just a few years, however, Newhart became a much more polished performer.)

His second album, *The Button-Down Mind Strikes Back,* was released late in 1960, and it turned out to be every bit as good as his first. In fact, the comedy on this album is more consistently amusing than on *The Button-Down Mind of Bob Newhart.* This second LP eventually sold over 500,000 copies, which was a very impressive figure in those days, although not quite as large a number as the sales for the first LP.

The critic for *Hi-Fi/Stereo Review* wrote in the March 1961 issue, "Bob Newhart's first album made some of us feel like

great discoverers. Now that he is one of the more popular comedians on records, this effort must be judged more in terms
of how good he seems the second time around. Happily, Newhart proves that he does indeed have staying power. His hesitant delivery, the aura of Mr. Average Guy that he creates, and
his ability to understate the most ludicrous remarks continue
to give him a special niche that distinguishes him from the
neurotics and sickniks among other leading comics."

By this point in Newhart's career, listeners had heard
enough of his material to get a good sense of what his humor
was all about. His antipathy towards large organizations is obvious on several of the routines on the second album. As befit-
ting a man who had spent a number of years working in
offices, Newhart often made fun of the kinds of things that go
on in bureaucracies. He might have looked like Mr. Average
Guy, but it was clear that he felt he didn't fit into any large
group.

"I resent large corporations," Newhart said in a 1962 interview. "They flatten personalities. When I worked for a huge
accounting firm, that was happening to me. So I quit. Besides,
I was a bum accountant. What gnaws me now is the concern
that if I become a show-business success, I may wind up being
a big operator myself. I'm fighting this."

James Conkling remembers Newhart's reluctance to discuss
business: "Bob does not like authority—as you know from listening to his records. Now Bob and I usually got along pretty
well. But when I tried to talk business with him, he'd suddenly turn very cool. He was always very friendly, except
when somebody who had authority over him wanted to get
him to do something."

Newhart says he has a particular aversion for "the personality tests given by some of the personnel departments of big corporations, so their company can staff itself with 'desirable young executive material.' What they're looking for is a guy who doesn't get out of line, who dresses conservatively, whose wife is compatible with the wives of the other executives—in short, a guy who thinks and reacts like a flat line on a graph. What knocks me out is that when they give one of those tests to the president of the corporation, he invariably flunks it. The president is usually a maverick. He's the one who thinks the unconventional thoughts that made the company grow. If he were a conformer, a member of the herd, his corporation wouldn't survive."

As Newhart sees it, the forms that people are now required to fill out for almost every occasion have become something like a great ocean that is threatening to drown the human race. "I hate filling out forms," he says. "In the fall of 1954, when I got out of the army, I entered Loyola University Law School. . . . The government was supposed to pay my tuition, and I kept waiting for the check to arrive. I'd been told that it would take a month and a half to reach me. Some of the other guys who got out of the army when I did received theirs, but I was being dunned by the college. Finally, I got a form from the Veterans Administration. On it someone had checked off the statement, 'The photostat of your marriage certificate is insufficient for our records.' I wasn't married—so naturally I hadn't sent them any photostat.

"I began to hate forms then. I hate them so much that I've fooled around with a routine in which a large corporation uses so many forms as a substitute for thinking that nobody in the corporation has to think at all. If the company has a problem which isn't covered by a form, that problem simply doesn't exist. What spoils everything is that some dopey character— me—pops up with a situation not covered by any of that corporation's forms. The guys in the office are so form-minded that rather than take care of my predicament, which is a tiny one, they band together and promise to support me if I'll go away and leave them alone."

"All of my stuff is full of anachronisms, a longing for the past, a less mechanical time," he explains.

The Button-Down Mind Strikes Back includes several amusing bits that deal with the subject of corporations. And, as might be expected, the corporations are thoroughly lampooned by Newhart. One of the most corrosive routines is "The Retirement Party," in which Newhart plays a man who has just been honored for fifty years of service to his firm. After listening to the usual dull speeches at the party (and after quite a few drinks), the man says, "I never heard such drivel. . . . I don't suppose it ever occurred to any of you that I had to get half-stoned every morning to get down to this crummy job. . . . You put in your fifty years, and all they ever give you is this crummy watch: I figure it works out to about twenty-eight cents a year. If it hadn't been for the fifty bucks a week I glommed out of petty cash, I couldn't have made it."

Regarding this routine, Newhart says, "Most retirement parties are shams. The ones I've attended certainly have been. My problem was how to have 'good old Charlie' stand up and say what he actually felt, instead of the phony things the departing one usually parrots. It seemed to me that it would be a healthy thing to have happen for a change. It also seemed to me the best way to have him tell the truth would be to have him a little drunk so he wouldn't care what he was saying."

Another entertaining track from the album is "A Private in Washington's Army," which is about the complaints of a foot soldier during the Revolutionary War: "You hear what Nutty George pulled last night? . . . The dollar across the Potomac, you didn't hear about that? . . . You know he had us out until three in the morning looking for the damn thing. . . . I finally got to sleep at five. . . . There was some nut flashing a light on and off in the church tower all night. . . . Then the minute he quits, this drunk goes riding through town screaming. . . . Here comes one of the real weirdos of them all— Benny . . . The one with the square glassses . . . Next time we have a thunderstorm, watch him."

"The Bus Driver's School" is superb. In this one, Newhart plays an instructor who teaches his students how to thwart an old lady running to catch a bus that's just pulling away from the curb. "See how he slammed the door right in her face that time!" the instructor says with enthusiasm. "That's known as your perfect pullout."

But best of all is "Ledge Psychology," an inspired bit of black humor. Making the subject of suicide seem funny is not easy, but Newhart manages to pull it off. He introduces the routine by explaining that modern police officers are told to adopt a casual, offhand manner in dealing with people who are threatening to leap off skyscraper ledges. Police manuals advise the officers not to wear a uniform, "since the image of authority may be just the reason they're out there to begin with." Also, the idea is to be totally unsympathetic and not plead with them in the expected way to "think of all they have to live for."

In the role of the modern policeman, Newhart steps out onto the ledge, notices the guy about to commit suicide, and casually greets him by saying, "Oh, hi." Next, Newhart's character denies that he's been sent there to talk the man out of killing himself. "You thinking about jumping, are you? Your first time, is it? . . . Me? No, no, I'm just on my way to work, as a matter of fact . . . I usually walk around on the ledges awhile, I think it kind of helps me unwind. . . . You know, you're drawing a hell of a crowd for a weekday. . . . Yeah, really. . . . You know, the last couple of years, jumping has really fallen off. . . . Oh, I'm sorry, I didn't mean it *that* way. . . . Seriously—you take 1929, for example. You literally couldn't get out on this ledge in 1929. . . . We had people lined up in the corridor just waiting to get out on the ledge. . . . We finally went to that numbered-card system they use in the butcher shops."

By early 1961 Newhart had become the most talked-about comedian in the country. If there were still any doubts about his new status, they were certainly dismissed when the Grammy awards for 1960 were handed out. *The Button-Down Mind of Bob Newhart* was given the award for being the "album of the year," *The Button-Down Mind Strikes Back* was given the Grammy for "best comedy performance," and Newhart was voted the "best new artist of the year."

On April 16, 1961, Newhart played to a packed auditorium at Carnegie Hall. In the next morning's edition of *The New York Times,* Arthur Gelb wrote that "for a man who has been exercising his twin talents of writing and acting for such a short time . . . he is an extraordinarily polished performer. He is also hilariously funny. . . . Mr. Newhart has a mild but astringent delivery that keeps you on the edge of your seat, when you are not figuratively rolling in the aisle."

Having triumphed on records, in nightclubs and concert halls, and in guest spots on TV, the next step for Newhart at this point in his career was inevitable. His next year would be even more hectic than the last, the pressures even more intense, and the expectations even higher.

4

"THE ONLY SATIRIST WORTH TALKING ABOUT" ON TV

Since he was then the hottest comedian in America, it wasn't especially surprising that Newhart was offered the chance to star in his own TV series. He turned CBS and ABC down, and chose NBC because they gave him a completely free hand.

Still, Newhart was at first reluctant to take the big step of having his own show. He was already having some misgivings about becoming overexposed on television through his frequent guest appearances. He wondered if he could work well with other writers and performers: before this, he'd always been on his own. And he worried that his appeal might not be broad enough. After all, a record was an enormous hit if it sold one million copies, but a television show would have to attract tens of millions of viewers. He certainly didn't want to be forced to "dumb it up" in order to reach a mass audience.

Finally, though, he decided to accept NBC's offer to host his own half-hour comedy/variety series for the 1961–1962 television season. "I don't think I'm going to be the savior of evening TV," he told a reporter for *Newsday* just before the premiere of the show. "I know I'm going to be up against a variety of other comics. . . . But TV is just something I think I ought to do. It was a case of my either standing still or taking a big gamble. If I hadn't taken a gamble a few years ago, I would still be an accountant." In the end, Newhart says, he realized that "if you're a pitcher, you'd better pitch in the major leagues."

For his producer, Newhart selected Roland Kibbee, a man who had been working in television and radio for twenty-five years. Kibbee first saw Newhart at the hungry i in San Francisco. According to Kibbee, "We got along fine initially. I thought, 'Here is a man who can do satire and not be heavy-handed about it.' I'd waited a long time since Fred Allen." Newhart says that Kibbee's enthusiasm was a big factor in his final decision to agree to host the show.

The first "Bob Newhart Show" premiered on October 11, 1961, and it was broadcast on Wednesdays at 10:00 P.M. during the 1961–1962 season. The program often began with an opening monologue by Newhart, in which he would sometimes come out holding a prop telephone. As usual with his routines, the audience would hear only his half of a telephone conversation. The monologues would normally end with him angrily saying "Same to you, fella!" and slamming down the receiver. Besides the monologues, "The Bob Newhart Show" featured a small group of comic actors and actresses who would appear in sketches with Newhart. Paul Weston and his orchestra provided most of the music, along with guest vocalists such as Jo Stafford and Nancy Wilson. But Newhart was on stage for almost the whole thirty minutes (he even did many of the commercials), and most of the humor was in the same vein as audiences were familiar with from his recordings. He tended to play the same kinds of characters on the show as he had done in his old routines.

A typical monologue, for example, from "The Bob Newhart Show" was a talk given by an instructor to a class for would-be moving men. (The resemblance between this bit and "The Bus Driver's School" from *The Button-Down Mind Strikes Back* is surely no coincidence.) Newhart's character says, "Okay, Johnson's getting ready to back the van in now. Fellas, you want to get off the lawn and come over on the driveway where you'll be safe? There he comes. . . . See, he got the mailbox. . . . There goes the picket fence . . . now the hedge . . . on the green in three. . . . Oh boy, look at those wheels dig into the lawn! . . . You see what he did there? That looks accidental, doesn't it? . . . See how he snapped off the sprinkler head? Golly, that gusher must be fifteen feet tall. . . . You fellas wanna be careful and take advantage of that mud there when you're going back and forth to the living room."

Newhart quickly learned that filling a half hour every week on TV was no easy matter. He was something of a worrier by nature anyway, and the job of supervising "The Bob Newhart Show" quickly became an enormous strain on him. What's more, we should bear in mind that at this point, Newhart had only worked in show business for about three years. It would be hard to imagine anyone phlegmatic enough (or dumb enough) not to have been more than a little anxious had they been in Newhart's shoes during the fall of 1961.

"TV's changed my life," Newhart told an interviewer for *TV Guide* magazine in January 1962. "I no longer have the luxury of laying an egg in front of two hundred people. Now if I lay one, it's in front of twenty-five or thirty million. But TV's taught me some things. Discipline. If your mind has to come up with just one new idea a month, it does that. If you need one a week, you can make it do that.

"For that reason, maybe it's been good. But I keep wondering how long I can last. . . . It *is* tough. We've had to depend on our own concepts, Kibbee and I. We had many $1,500-a-week writers come and tell us how they were dying to work, how they couldn't wait to do that take-off on 'The Untouchables.' Who needs that?"

At first, Newhart tried to play a wide variety of different characters in the sketches on his show. But soon he discovered that audiences weren't responding favorably to some of his portrayals. "I found out some things about my acting ability I never realized," he explains. "TV's taught me I can't play a schnook. We had one sketch about a guy caught without money as he's checking out of a hotel, trying to avoid giving tips. It didn't come off." And ever since his experience with his first variety show, Newhart has been careful not to take on roles that are clearly outside of his dramatic range. He's a first-rate comedian, and irresistibly funny at what he does well, but Newhart knows that if he plays a part that is wrong for him, audiences won't accept it. As a Romeo, for instance, someone like Bob Newhart is hardly going to cut a dashing figure.

With Newhart supervising their efforts, four writers were initially selected to come up with the material for the show: Kibbee, Bob Kaufman, Charles Sherman, and Norman Leibman. This group would produce a script between Monday and Wednesday of each week. On Thursdays, the cast held an informal run-through, on Fridays and Saturdays rehearsals took place in the NBC studios in Burbank, and on Saturday evenings the final result was filmed before an audience. Sixteen-hour days were common for members of the cast and crew on those hectic days at the end of the week.

Newhart made a decision to avoid using his old routines from his albums on the new show. He found that on those few occasions when he did use them, he got a number of complaints from people who wondered if he was running out of material. Of course, this only increased the pressures on Newhart and his writers.

Letters from viewers soon started arriving by the hundreds, often including suggestions for how Newhart could supposedly improve the show. "Half the suggestions were much too dirty," he says. "Then when they get through telling you their brilliant ideas, they say, 'I guess you're going to have to clean this up a little bit.'

"Then there are the people who have wonderful ideas about which guest stars you ought to have. They tell you you ought to get Victor Borge. I wish I could have afforded to hire Victor Borge."

In fact, Newhart was getting so many suggestions in the mail that lawyers advised him to take precautions against the

eventuality that somebody might sue him for allegedly stealing
their ideas. What he did, then, was always have someone else
on his staff open any envelope that contained more than one
sheet of paper, since those envelopes might have scripts or
monologues in them.

From the beginning, the Nielsen ratings for "The Bob
Newhart Show" were good, but unspectacular; there seemed
little chance it would soon crack the top ten. Critically, however, the show fared better, with most reviewers finding it to
be much better written and performed than the typical com-
edy/variety program.

"Careful attention to the fundamental values of American
life, all too rare on the tiny screen, is the salient feature of 'The
Bob Newhart Show.'" said *Newsweek* in the January 15, 1962
issue. "The progenitor of all this wisdom doesn't look like
much—scrawny frame, shifty eyes, receding hairline—and the
effectiveness of his labors varies enormously, but thirty-two-
year-old Bob Newhart is still the only satirist worth talking
about in all television."

Several of the critics called Newhart an "intellectual," a label which he says may be misleading. "I'm not sure it's accurate. I guess it comes from my saying on occasion that I've
read a book. I suppose if you read, that makes you brilliant. I
don't think of myself as an intellectual. My interests are var-
ied, and I tend to read whatever I'm curious about."

In his review for *TV Guide,* Gilbert Seldes's opinion was
that "The Bob Newhart Show" "takes your intelligence for
granted" and that it had "a sound and an atmosphere which
have almost vanished from the air." Seldes pointed out that "if
he [Newhart] takes a swipe at the free enterprise system by

showing how a private fire department would work, it is the almost unbearable patience he displays that provides the fun and the satire. There is a kind of tension as the basic joke is stretched just far enough for Newhart to give you at the end his brief and winning smile."

Not all the notices were quite so favorable, however. Writing in the *Village Voice,* Martin William called Newhart "a sick comic for middlebrows." William commented, "I wish everybody would come off it about Bob Newhart. He is a pleasant comedian. But surely the fact that his fairly affable jibes at business and politics have been called 'penetrating' and 'outspoken' is a symptom of something more than the usual carelessness with which the word 'satire' is slung around. I wonder whom he is supposed to offend." William, it seems, fell into the trap of confusing Newhart's mild-mannered style of delivery with the actual content of the sketches themselves, which often had some very pointed, though not necessarily obvious, things to say.

Seen today, the first "Bob Newhart Show" holds up pretty well, although it is admittedly uneven. The best parts of the show are certainly on a par with many of the routines on Newhart's albums; in fact, some bits wound up being recorded for Warner Brothers Records soon afterward.

One thing that's obvious right away is that Newhart worked much better alone than he did with other actors and actresses. We don't see much evidence of the dependable smoothie who reacts so well on the sitcoms of the seventies and eighties. Instead Newhart is more high-strung, more intense, and, often, plainly nervous. He is forever straightening his tie, and his voice often soars up to a high falsetto range when things aren't going well.

Yet when he simply stands still and gives one of his monologues directly into the camera, he does a solid, professional job of it. The sketches, on the other hand, are a mixed bag—many are amateurish, sort of like The Mighty Carson Art Players from "The Tonight Show." In these bits, Newhart tends to rely too much on using funny-sounding voices and unusual accents. His supporting cast rarely seems much better than your typical dinner theater troupe.

What's best about the show is that it was one of the first programs to mock the conventions of television. Like "Late Night with David Letterman" today, the old "Bob Newhart Show" included a lot of self-parody. Newhart's variety program had a hip sensibility that was ahead of its time, and must have been an influence on shows such as "Laugh-In" and "The Smothers Brothers Comedy Hour" in the late sixties.

For instance, at the beginning of one show Newhart comes out and tells the audience, "We've discussed several times in the past how important *warmth* is to a television show. A couple of months ago we mentioned that a surefire way of generating warmth is to hold a small child on stage while you're doing . . . anything. We also discussed how you could give the illusion of warmth by talking to members of the crew on a first-name basis. And a couple weeks ago Carl Reiner and I did a kind of warm thing, I think, in singing our respective high-school songs, which would fall into the general category of nostalgia—or maybe nausea. Now there's a further danger, and that is in becoming so warm you're no longer human. In the next few weeks you may notice less warmth on the show, but I think you'll find more humanness."

Some of the funniest moments of the program are Newhart's introductions of his guests and the comments Newhart makes as master of ceremonies, in between the sketches. Before Jack Paar makes his appearance on the show, Newhart says to the audience, "I'm sure that Jack introduces his guests more glowingly than anyone else. He's the only man on television who has separate sponsors for his introductions." And then Newhart tells this story: "Once I was waiting backstage to go on one of Jack's shows. Waiting with me were Buddy Hackett, Joey Bishop, and Jack Leonard. And, of course, on Jack's show you never know when you'll be called out. Then we heard Jack's voice saying, 'Ladies and gentlemen, the individual I'm about to introduce is mankind's greatest benefactor. The most inspiring public figure of our time. A personage whose wit and wisdom have illuminated the darkest corners of our globe. Ladies and gentlemen,' said Jack, 'here truly is a living saint.' And, of course, the four of us rushed out—leaving Dr. Albert Schweitzer standing backstage. As it turned out, though, Jack was introducing Zsa Zsa Gabor."

Many of the routines on the show are based on cleverly thought-out premises. One time Newhart plays a traffic expert hired by a small town to bring in some extra revenue. Newhart's character devises an elaborate speed trap, with "judges riding piggyback on motorcycles" so that the unfortunate drivers could just "pay and go." On another occasion Newhart portrays a bank officer who refuses to loan money to a man who wants to build the Great Pyramid. The bank officer frowns and says, "That foundation doesn't seem too substantial to me." But then we see that he is holding a drawing of the pyramid upside down.

Although the quality of "The Bob Newhart Show" appeared

to be improving as the season went along, and Newhart was plainly becoming more confident and polished in his delivery, behind the scenes there were problems that were growing worse. Frictions were developing between Newhart and his team of producers and writers. Newhart found himself disagreeing often with the judgments of his staff.

"I started with the frivolous notion that we could be a team," Roland Kibbee said. "But he (Newhart) is not a team man. . . . It soon became a question of his putting his career in my hands—or mine in his. That I was unwilling to do."

The conflicts between Newhart and Kibbee soon became irreconcilable. "Kib is a strong man," Newhart says. "He had been writing comedy for twenty-five years and I'd been at it only three or four. So he figured, rightly, 'Who's this guy to tell me?' Of course, I figured I'd been writing for Bob Newhart three years longer than Kib had.

"So tremendous pressure built up. We collected wastebaskets full of discarded material. I'd say, 'I'm not too wild about this line.' He'd say, 'I think it's funny.' One of us had to compromise. That's something I haven't learned to do yet."

Newhart was discovering the great difference between writing for his comedy albums and writing for a weekly television series. "In a nightclub you have control," he explains. "You can polish your material. In TV you do it without knowing whether it'll turn out funny or not. Then . . . it's gone. I began to feel, I'm not a comedian, I'm a corporation. And then—you die a little every week."

Newhart recalls that "Kibbee'd bring in a script and I'd want to change it—make it more 'like me.' I was comfortable with the monologues, but the sketches were tough. My comedy wasn't ideally suited for television; it depended too much on what you didn't see."

What made matters especially troublesome was that many of the people then working on "The Bob Newhart Show" had been selected for their jobs by Kibbee—and among this group was Coby Ruskin, the director. (Newhart calls Ruskin "a director who wanted broader comedy than I'm able to deliver.")

In February 1962 Kibbee resigned from the show, followed shortly by Ruskin and several of the writers. Newhart then asked Ralph Levy, who had previously worked with Jack Benny, to replace Kibbee. "MCA brought half a dozen [directors] around," remembers Newhart. "I liked Levy's ideas best." During the last few months, Levy is listed as both the producer and the director of "The Bob Newhart Show."

"We wanted to get more of a sense of a smooth flow into the show," explains Levy. "I didn't try to make a lot of big changes. . . . But we did want a closer relationship between Bob and the guests. A faster pace. Bigger production."

One of the writers who resigned from the program was Bob Kaufman. He says he quit when he was asked to because "I kept fighting to do satirical comedy and hitting at sacred cows . . . and Newhart didn't want satire on the show." Kaufman admits that "Newhart can ad-lib, and did. He's the best monologuist I've ever seen, but . . . Bob was pretty timid about doing shows about the hate groups. . . . Our sponsors gave us no trouble, they liked satire, but our star didn't."

One reason why Newhart was having differences with his writers was that his brand of comedy was much more subtle than what is usually seen on TV. Newhart's routines on his LPs are full of satire, but it is satire of a wry, discerning kind.

There are no overt political messages in Newhart's humor. He doesn't set up easy targets. He would never knock down a door with a battering ram when he could quietly pick the lock to achieve the same result.

What Newhart learned from his experience on his first show was the vital importance of surrounding himself with people who share his point of view about comedy. Even if someone is very talented and has lots of impressive credentials, he still must think the same way about the project as his co-workers— or else they are all headed for discord. On his sitcoms, Newhart has been careful never to let that unharmonious situation develop again. His staffs on the recent shows have been filled only with people that he's completely comfortable being around.

During the spring of 1962, "The Bob Newhart Show" seemed to be running more smoothly than before. The ratings were still respectable, though average, and the program was nominated for several Emmies. So it came as something of a surprise when NBC and the sponsors, for reasons which were never made particularly clear, decided not to renew "The Bob Newhart Show" for the next season. The last episode was telecast June 13, 1962; it was the thirty-ninth show of the series. (In those days a TV season was much more substantial than it is today. In the eighties most series can get by with only twenty-two or twenty-four episodes per year.)

Ironically, "The Bob Newhart Show" wound up winning more awards than any of Newhart's sitcoms, even though it was so short-lived. The show won the prestigious Peabody award and also an Emmy for being the "outstanding program achievement in the field of humor" for the 1961–1962 TV season.

"I'm probably the only guy ever to get a Peabody award, an Emmy, and a pink slip all in one year," Newhart comments, "and so it made me a little gun-shy of ever doing another series."

Furthermore, Newhart says that "I think I may have been a little more bitter than I realized. I'm finding out now that it did have an effect on me. My pride was offended, naturally, but I said, 'At last the pressure's off and I can relax.' And I did. I felt I owed it to myself. But I remember thinking, 'What the hell? What's the use of trying?' So I guess I was bitter all right."

In retrospect, Newhart offers this description of the experience of doing his first show: "It was like trying to fly a plane without knowing what makes it go. I had this hang-up about perfection; I guess I always had it. But I knew nothing about my craft. I was raw funny, not polished funny. Deep down I guess I didn't feel entitled to all that success."

With the big pressure off him, Newhart had a chance to begin leading a personal life again. For the past two and a half years he had been so busy he scarcely had had time to think about anything other than coming up with his next comedy routine. And he also had the opportunity to consider what he wanted to do next with his career. His show was off the air, but he was still one of the country's top entertainers—and he was only thirty-two years old.

5 | NEW DIRECTIONS

The next few years following the cancellation of his first TV series were filled with new ventures for Newhart: He got married, appeared in his first movie, made more record albums, starred in another TV series, and continued to perform regularly on variety shows hosted by Garry Moore, Jack Paar, Ed Sullivan, and many others.

"When the show failed," remembers Newhart, "I was shaken. Everything till then had worked. Maybe I was a flash in the pan. I panicked. Like Peggy Lee, I asked myself, 'Is that all there is?' I developed doubts about things. I had this mortal fear of drunks and hecklers. When I played the clubs I used to peer out from behind the curtains hoping to spot the belligerent ones, looking for some peculiarity I could use to get back at them. It didn't work; I never seemed to pick the right ones."

Newhart had always had a tendency to be anxious about his future, to worry a bit more than necessary about his prospects. (Perhaps this was partly a product of his strict upbringing, in which he was sometimes made to feel more than his share of guilt and anxiety.) Newhart was now famous, but he had just suffered the first real setback of his career when "The Bob Newhart Show" was taken off the air. His situation gave rise to a whole new set of worries, which he would have found completely unimaginable three years before. He no longer had to be concerned about coming up with enough money to pay the phone bill or be afraid that he couldn't get a date. Yet Newhart found he still had plenty of new things to worry about.

Such as remaining the hottest comedian on television. "I used to sit down every Sunday night and watch 'The Ed Sullivan Show,'" Newhart recalls. "I'd watch the comedians and every week I'd say to the TV set, 'Well, fella, you're okay, but not socko. We know who's still number one.' Then one night I turned on the show and there was a guy named Bill Cosby. 'Good luck, kid,' I said. 'Take it and run with it awhile.'"

Another source of concern was that he would lose touch with his roots: "I was in a heck of a spot really, trying to relate again to things I used to relate to when I was an accountant. . . . It's a danger all comedians face. You have to keep in mind what it was that first propelled you to be funny. What happens is you become more affluent, you get an apartment in Hollywood, you start going around with a horsey set, and pretty soon you lose sight of people's problems. . . . A comedian has to keep being involved."

After his variety show was taken off the air, Newhart's fans next got a chance to see him in *Hell Is for Heroes,* which was released in July 1962. (Newhart had gone before the cameras for this film the previous summer.) He played a prissy army headquarters clerk, Private Driscoll, in this World War II picture.

The star of *Hell Is for Heroes* was Steve McQueen, who gave a strong performance as a surly American soldier named John Reese. Reese is a social misfit, almost a misanthrope under ordinary circumstances, but when the fighting begins he shows himself to be an extraordinary soldier.

The film was directed by Don Siegel in a plain, straightforward style. The performances and script all contribute toward achieving an atmosphere of gritty realism. The only drawback is that so much of what happens soon becomes predictable: the film is mostly ninety minutes' worth of seeing grim-faced men going about their military duties.

Newhart provides some badly needed comic relief with his portrayal of meek Private Driscoll. Driscoll gets lost while driving a shipment of typewriters to division headquarters. An outfit of soldiers then decides to commandeer his jeep for their own needs. Driscoll is incensed, but his protests are ineffectual:

DRISCOLL: Sarge, wait a minute.

SERGEANT: Don't worry about Major Winston. He'll be mighty happy you volunteered for combat duty.

DRISCOLL: You don't understand. I was sent to clerk-typist school. All I've ever done in the army is type.

SERGEANT: Then we're gonna be giving you some on-the-job training.

So Driscoll joins the outfit, albeit reluctantly. The men are in desperate need of more soldiers, but it's questionable whether

Driscoll is an asset or a liability. He even has to be taught how to use a rifle properly.

Hell Is for Heroes was praised by many of the critics, but audiences weren't quite as enthusiastic. *The New York Times*'s reviewer wrote that it was "an unusually well-made film." And he said that "Harry Guardino, Bob Newhart, James Coburn, and Joseph Hoover are GI's true to the life."

Newsweek's reviewer commented, *"Hell Is for Heroes* manages, thanks to its sharp script and incisive direction, to look like a film about soldiers instead of actors."

The ending of *Hell Is for Heroes,* in which the Steve Mc-Queen character performs some amazing heroics, seems curiously abrupt. The reason for this, explains Newhart, is not that the director was deliberately trying to be "arty," but because of problems with the budget. "We spent a few weeks wandering around the hills of Northern California," he recalls, "then Paramount refused to spend any more money on it, and the film just ended."

Newhart was still single at this time, though he was by no means a confirmed bachelor. "I would like someone to share all this with," he told a columnist for the New York *Mirror* in April 1961. "Part of it is lost being alone. . . . But I move from town to town, and even if I meet a nice girl, there's always that [problem]."

He was introduced in 1961 to Virginia Quinn, who was then an actress, by an unlikely matchmaker, Buddy Hackett. Ginny was a vivacious redhead with green eyes and a model's figure—and she wasn't, at first, all that taken with Newhart. "When we first began dating," she remembers, "he figured bells should be ringing and sirens going off. I guess it was more that way for him than for me because I continued to date another man."

Bob and Ginny soon decided, however, that they appreciated each other too much to let each other go. They found that they had many qualities in common and that they also complemented each other in many important ways. Bob was soft-spoken and reserved, while Ginny was a high-spirited, nonstop conversationalist. Bob was totally disorganized when it came to planning things, while Ginny was the reverse. Bob was messy; Ginny, neat. Part of Ginny's role in the relationship soon became to soothe Bob's anxieties and to help arrange his social calendar for him.

But, Ginny admits, she had her doubts about the relationship right up until their marriage in 1963. "Bob was always so *sure,* but when I walked down the aisle at St. Victor's Church I was so nervous that my veil was shaking. My father whispered, 'Sweetheart, I can still get you out of this.' But I've never regretted our marriage one minute, not even when I blast out Bob's closet, or he teases me about what he calls my Planned Activity Time—or when he complains that the house is so neat it looks as though we're expecting real estate brokers to come through."

Bob's messiness is a subject for considerable contention around the Newhart household. "He never hangs up anything," says Ginny. "And you should see him going off to work. He insists on wearing corduroy slacks that are too short and have been pressed so often they're shiny. And sneakers. Recently I threw out three pairs with holes in them. I say to him, 'You know, you're the star of your own show. Button your shirt.' But Bob hates to shop for clothes and he couldn't care less about what he wears.

"We don't argue very much, we just sort of kid on the square. It takes a lot to get him riled up, but when he really loses his temper—he has a bit of German blood, so I say 'Achtung!' and he says, "But I'm mostly Irish!'

"One of our arguments was about golf. He left home at ten in the morning and called at seven when dinner was burning in the oven. He said he was still at the club, and I said even thirty-six holes of golf didn't take nine hours—and he could stay at the club if he loved it so much. He's never done that again, and although I don't play golf I don't feel widowed. I'm even sorry he has so little time for it now because of the show."

Ginny has been waging a campaign for years to overcome Bob's lack of interest in food. She says, "On our first real date he took me to dinner. I ordered chicken salad and he ordered [nothing but] a drink, and sat there and stared at me while I ate. It was terrible, his watching my every move. I was so nervous I spilled mayonnaise on my purple dress, and then he announced we were going to drop in on the Carl Reiners. I'd never met them and I was scared and held my purse over the spot on my dress. I could have killed Bob.

"Then, just after we were married, he gave me a list of things he didn't eat—pork chops, veal, lamb chops, et cetera. He weighed a hundred and forty-seven then, and I figured no one could hate *all* those things, so I camouflaged pork chops in mushroom soup and he commented that it was good chicken. Then with the children growing up he had to set an example, so by now he eats like a human being. And weighs a lot more than a hundred and forty-seven."

Ginny feels that she has helped Bob in many different

ways to take a more relaxed approach to life. For instance, over the years he has learned to enjoy performing much more than he used to. "The first time I caught his act, I couldn't bear to watch," she remembers. "He was really uptight about the drunks. He'd hassle the maître d's, trying to get them to do something about it. Later, he began to realize he could cope. Then one night, after a bout with a heckler, he came off saying, 'Gee, that's the most fun I've had in years.'"

Those who know the Newharts say that their marriage seems to be a very good one. Suzanne Pleshette says that "Ginny is so right for Bob. What they both are today is the result . . . of years of loving and living, and many of his attractive qualities are those that have flowered in his marriage to Ginny."

And Mary Tyler Moore says, "I have often seen Bob and Ginny on the tennis courts at the club we all belong to—and, you know, you can't help liking a man who so obviously loves his wife."

Soon after their marriage, Bob and Ginny bought a lovely house in Beverly Hills, where they planned to begin raising a family. They've since had four children—Robert, twenty-four; Timothy, twenty-one; Jennifer, seventeen; and Courtney, ten. Because Bob and Ginny each grew up in strict Catholic households, they have brought up their children as Catholics, too— but with a difference. "We don't want the children to have the fears that were instilled in us," explains Ginny.

The Newhart household has always been very child-centered, with toys scattered about, pets in evidence, and a playhouse built next to the paddleball court.

Ginny describes Bob as a devoted father, although she admits that "at first Bob couldn't bring himself to discipline the children. And in those days he was away so much on club dates that I finally had to explain that I needed his help when he was home. . . . Later, he was fine with the boys, but I have to face it, he'll *never* discipline Jennifer or Courtney. . . . When somebody once asked him how he'll react when her [Jennifer's] boy friends start coming around, he said, 'Jennifer is going to be a wealthy spinster.'"

Ginny recalls that their oldest son, Robert (born on December 4, 1963), was sick a great deal when he was little, so that he wound up missing a considerable amount of school. At one point counselors advised the Newharts to send Robert to a school in New Hampshire, where he could make up for lost time. And Rob did so well there he eventually won a number of scholastic honors.

The Newharts have never gone in for much socializing, though they do attend an occasional Hollywood function. They tend to prefer a small group of friends they are very familiar with. Bob especially enjoys the company of other comedians, such as Dick Martin, Buddy Hackett, and Don Rickles.

Bob Newhart and Don Rickles are, at least so far as their public images are concerned, total opposites. Rickles is abrasive in the extreme; his humor consists mainly of outrageous insults. Newhart, on the other hand, is always soft-spoken. And yet Newhart and Rickles are best friends.

They first met in Las Vegas. Shortly afterward, Rickles introduced Bob and Ginny from the stage during one of his stand-up routines by saying the Newharts were "that stammering idiot from Chicago and his wife, the former hooker from St. Louis." Newhart says that despite Rickles's endless insults, he's actually a very softhearted guy.

Newhart jokes that "when you're friends with Rickles you don't pay attention to what he's saying. It's like music; it's in the background and you hear it, but it's kind of a loud din. Because if you listen to everything he says, you'd be exhausted. So you occasionally tune in and catch the thread of it, and then you tune out."

"I love the guy," says Rickles. "He's Mr. America in a crowd. Charlie Everybody, the American flag with a ribbon tied around him. Not Jewish, not Italian. I'm different. I don't live and relive everything I do on stage. I come from a Jewish family where men kissed. Shook up Bob. I remember the first time I embraced him. It was like holding on to an ice cake."

Don Rickles's wife Barbara explains that Newhart is much more outgoing when he's with them than he is with many other people. "He's a lot more sociable around his home than Don is around ours," she says. "We have the most fun when we're with Bob and Ginny. Together we've gone to Hawaii, Italy, Mexico, and on a Caribbean Cruise."

Newhart agrees that "with friends, with my very close friends, I'm different. Like with Rickles . . . we just have a great time going back and forth, and it isn't all Don. But I still have a natural reticence with most people, unlike Don, who is just the opposite. He'll go up to a total stranger and do twenty minutes."

Newhart didn't stop making his comedy albums after he began hosting his TV show. In 1962 he put out *Behind the*

Button-Down Mind and *The Button-Down Mind On TV;* in 1964 there was *Bob Newhart Faces Bob Newhart;* in 1965, *The Windmills Are Weakening;* and in 1967, *This Is It!* (These albums were all released by Warner Brothers Records.)

Unfortunately, the sales of each album tended to be less than the previous one, and the reviewers tended to become more negative as time went on. Yet the quality of most of Newhart's routines remained on the same level as before. The best explanation for Newhart's decline in popularity is that people were no longer finding his style to be a novelty; they felt they were familiar with the kind of comedy he was performing. And there's no question that he did overexpose himself on television during the years 1960, 1961, and 1962. Moreover, it must be remembered that reviewers have a tendency to praise an artist in glowing terms when he first becomes famous, then knock him off his pedestal later.

Behind the Button-Down Mind features several fine Newhart efforts, including one routine about an encounter between Khrushchev and an ordinary American. Newhart explains that "I got to thinking . . . there could be a certain kind of crisis if a typical American tourist were to meet Khrushchev at the UN."

Newhart's character in the monologue greets the Soviet leader by saying, "Hi, aren't you—don't tell me—you're Nicky Khrushchev, aren't you? . . . The wife and I have seen you on television. . . . We're just in town for the weekend. . . . I hear you're in town for the talks. . . . You know, I was reading in the papers about it. Now what do you clowns want with West Berlin, anyway?"

The Newhart character, who is a tourist from Iowa, asks

Khrushchev to pose for some gag photos with his wife, Martha, and his son, Brucey. For the picture Martha pretends to be swooning in Khrushchev's arms. "You know, the Rudolph Valentino thing," says Newhart's character. "Nicky, get a little fire in your eyes. . . . Yeah, I know she's not that great. . . . The folks back home will never believe this." At the end, the tourist from Iowa beats Khrushchev at arm wrestling, and Khrushchev gets upset and smashes the camera.

The reviewer for the *American Record Guide* wrote, "In *Behind the Button-Down Mind* he [Newhart] manages to squeeze some humor out of such familiar topics as a children's show (he depicts the whole sordid fraud with merciless devastation), TV commercials, travelogues, and no less a sacred target than Herb Philbrick, the FBI spy who started out exposing the Communists among whom he roamed incognito, and later turned into a shrill fanatic on his own."

The best-known routine on Newhart's next LP, *The Button-Down Mind On TV,* is called "Introducing Tobacco to Civilization." Newhart introduces this bit by saying, "Milestones are never really recognized right away. It takes fifty or sixty years before people realize what an achievement it is. Take, for instance, tobacco. It was discovered by Sir Walter Raleigh, and he sent it over to England from the colonies. Now it seems to me that the uses for tobacco aren't obvious right off the bat."

And so Newhart imagines a phone conversation between Sir Walter Raleigh and the head of the West Indies Company back in England. Sir Walter attempts to explain why he's sent over a huge shipment of this strange plant: "What is it this time, Walt? You got another winner for us, do ya? . . . To-bac-co? . . . What's tobacco, Walt? . . . It's a kind of leaf? . . .

And you bought eighty tons of it? . . . What are some of its uses, Walt? . . . You can chew it, or put it in a pipe, or you can shred it up . . . and put it on a piece of paper and roll it up and—don't tell me, Walt, don't tell me—you stick it in your ear, right Walt? . . . Oh, between your lips. . . . Then what do you do with it? . . . You set fire to it? . . . Then what do you do? . . . You inhale the smoke? . . . It seems offhand like you could stand over your fireplace and get the same effect. . . . See, Walt, we've been getting a little worried about you—ever since you put your cape down over that mud."

Another clever bit on the album concerns a man who visits a friend, only to be terrorized by his host's ferocious (and enormous) pet dog. Newhart explains that it occurred to him that many people have been in this situation of "being invited to someone's house, and they've had this dog since it was a puppy. They think of it as still being a puppy, but it is now a large, vicious dog. You're sort of on the horns of a dilemma because you don't want to offend your host, but at the same time you don't want to get eaten." As the dog progressively chews up the Newhart character's clothes and limbs, he keeps saying, "Hi fella, hi boy." The man's efforts to restrain the dog are all futile, however, and he becomes more and more desperate, with the result that the listener becomes more and more amused.

In one routine Newhart portrays a man presiding over a sales meeting of the "General Chariot Corporation" of ancient Rome. He informs us that "a lot of dealers have been complaining about the little chariot the Huns have come out with, so we're putting out a compact model of our own with the horses in the rear. It gives the driver a better view."

The reviewer for *High Fidelity* commented that on this album Newhart "satirizes the mores of our time not through a funny way of talking, but through the sharp and merciless spotlight of his probing wit." The *American Record Guide,* on the other hand, said that "the problem [with *The Button-Down Mind On TV*] is that Newhart has chosen too narrow a range of operations, and his own honesty does not seem fierce enough any more to give teeth to his treatment of liars, cheats, and assorted confidence men of the respectable world."

In 1964 Newhart agreed to return to TV on a regular basis as one of the co-hosts, along with Carol Burnett and Caterina Valente, of the CBS variety series "The Entertainers." Considering the number of talented people involved with the show, it might seem surprising that "The Entertainers" bombed in the ratings, but, Newhart explains, the project was in fact doomed from the start. "They put me and Carol and Caterina and Dom DeLuise together," says Newhart, "and that was a disaster. None of us had come of age, and we certainly didn't belong together."

"The Entertainers" first went on the air on Friday, September 25, 1964, at 8:30 P.M. (In January, CBS moved the show to Saturday evenings at 9:00 P.M.) The format was unusual, to say the least, and must have caused more than its share of confusion for the viewers, scarce though they were. The idea was that each of the three stars would have at least one week off every month. Sometimes all three were in evidence; sometimes, only two; and sometimes, only one.

It shouldn't have taken a programming genius to figure out

that "The Entertainers" would soon become, in the words of *TV Guide,* a "videoland disaster area." *Variety*'s reviewer wrote, "'The Entertainers' . . . just seemed to ramble along aimlessly and pointlessly, lacking any distinct class or style and undecided which way it wanted to go."

The producers started to book a number of rock groups for appearances on the show, in an attempt to lure the younger viewers. Newhart was not at all pleased by this move. One of the reasons he gave later for quitting "The Entertainers" was that the audiences were becoming too young to understand his jokes. "I mentioned Werner von Braun in one routine," he remembers, "and it was obvious from the response that few in the audience had heard of him."

Carol Burnett offers these thoughts about the show's demise: "Well, you're always hoping for a smash hit, and this wasn't it. It wasn't really publicized enough. At the start, the show had no focal point, such as a Garry Moore. And 'The Addams Family,' which we were opposite then—a show with marvelous teenage appeal—came on the air two weeks before us."

Newhart abandoned ship at the beginning of 1965, and the show was canceled two months later. The last episode was shown on March 27, 1965.

Still, Newhart remembers that the experience of making "The Entertainers" was not entirely unpleasant. He says he is proud of some of the jokes and sketches he did on the program, even if no one laughed. He recalls, for instance, that "I did one routine on a civilian who had gone up to Mars so that people outside the space program could relate to it. Of course, the first question he was asked when he returned was, 'What are the people like up there? Is it a more advanced civilization?' And he said, 'Yes, it's more advanced.' And then they asked, 'Well, how much more advanced would you say it is?' He said, 'I'd say it was six or eight weeks ahead . . . I noticed they had disposable razors up there, and we didn't have them until about six weeks later.'

"I loved that," Newhart says. "But it just went nowhere."

6 | "THE LEAN YEARS"

Newhart remained a familiar face on TV during the rest of the sixties, even though he wasn't starring in any series at that time. He made guest appearances on variety shows such as "The Hollywood Palace" and "The Smothers Brothers Comedy Hour," and he occasionally accepted spots on sitcoms and game shows. (Only a true Newhart trivia expert could recall some of these obscure performances, such as his part in a 1967 episode of the short-lived NBC series "Captain Nice," which starred William Daniels as a police chemist who invents "Super Juice" and becomes a crime-fighting hero along the lines of Batman and Superman.)

But Newhart's most important role on television in the mid to late sixties was on "The Tonight Show." He was the guest host on seventy-eight occasions, and it was on this show that he perfected his smoother, more genial style before the cameras. In his earlier television performances, Newhart had always appeared to be a little nervous and high-strung, but by the late sixties he was clearly developing into the master of mellow that we know today.

Still, he found it to be a difficult period because his audiences seemed mostly to want to hear him repeat his old comedy material. Newhart went on the road four months a year, playing nightclubs and concert halls, and he took his family with him wherever he traveled. "I didn't starve," he says of that period, "but I guess you could call them the lean years."

He played Las Vegas frequently, commanding as much as $35,000 per week (which should have kept the Newhart family from becoming too lean). According to Newhart, performing in Las Vegas is never enjoyable. "Part of Vegas is energy. They don't care if you're good or bad if they can say, 'He or she really works hard.' For the money they pay, they want to see somebody sweat. And if you don't sweat, they don't think you've entertained them. . . . After you've played there about five weeks, you literally don't know what day it is." Newhart explains that in the middle of one of his Vegas appearances he often gets the feeling on stage that he has already given the very same monologue a few minutes before, that "I'm telling the same joke and that's why they're staring at me—because they just heard this joke. And then they laugh and you realize, 'No, I told it in the first show.' But you still have this terrible feeling."

Undoubtedly Newhart found this period to be, in many ways, a frustrating one, yet he did manage to ride the roller coaster of success—and misfortunes—well. He kept plugging away with his show-business career, even though there must have been moments, especially after "The Entertainers" flopped, when he must have been tempted to chuck it all for a few years. But he was never one to give in totally to feelings of depression or discouragement. And he was certainly not one to

drown his troubles in drink or drugs. Nobody describes Newhart as someone who was prone to dissipating himself in
gluttonous excesses of the flesh. His only excesses, apparently,
were in drinking too many Pepsi-Colas and playing too much
golf.

As time passed Newhart says he began to notice that audiences were no longer responding to his monologues in quite
the same way. He discovered that many people seemed to have
shorter attention spans. "I began to find that audiences
wouldn't sit still for those long six- and eight-minute monologues. They wanted it short and precise, so I had to do something." He says he began to be "more conversational" in his
act rather than simply reciting his set routines. "The audience
wants to feel they're watching something that you are relating
to them, which makes them part of the show," he explains.

During the sixties Newhart was involved in several campaigns for Democratic Party candidates. He was an especially
strong supporter of the Kennedys. Although Newhart is by no
means an extreme left-winger, he says the idea of a reactionary
comic is "a contradiction in terms." In his opinion, "There's
no Republican Mort Sahl. Can't be. Anybody as individual as a
comic would naturally tend toward the liberal party."

Despite his involvement with Democratic campaigns, politics has rarely played a part in Newhart's humor. "I don't
think a performer should give answers," he says. "You can run
out of targets for political satire and find yourself forced into
artificial attitudes for laughs."

This doesn't mean, Newhart explains, that he doesn't have
strong opinions and feelings about the world around him—
just that certain feelings are difficult to express in terms of

comedy. "Comedians have great anger," he says. "I have to check myself constantly when I feel that anger rising in me. I get most furious over people's inconsiderateness to other people, all forms of inconsiderateness. I suppose I'm too much the other way, but if I weren't I couldn't live with myself."

In 1965 Warner Brothers Records released *The Windmills Are Weakening,* which turned out to be one of Newhart's finest comedy albums. The sales of the record were poor and the critical reaction was mainly negative, but it featured some outstanding routines, including "King Kong" and "Superman and the Dry Cleaner."

"King Kong" concerns the troubles of a guard working at the Empire State Building on the night that King Kong climbed up. The guard, who's only just been hired that day, attempts to report the situation to his boss:

"This isn't your standard ape, sir. He's between eighteen and nineteen stories high, depending on whether there's a thirteenth floor or not. . . . I got a broom without signing a requisition for it. . . . I will tomorrow, yes sir. . . . And I started hitting him on the toe with it. It didn't bother him much . . . and he's carrying a woman in his hand, sir. . . . No, I don't think she works in the building, no sir. . . . She has a kind of a negligee on, so I doubt very much she's one of the cleaning women."

In "Superman and the Dry Cleaner" we hear about the plight of Clark Kent, who is unable to fly to the rescue of Lois Lane because of a mix-up at the cleaners. Newhart introduces this bit by saying, "We've all gone through this situation of when you send out a suit to the cleaners and get the wrong suit back. It's not a major inconvenience usually, but supposing Superman got the wrong suit back from the cleaners. Now he would have a problem."

Newhart then imagines that Lois Lane is being held by kidnappers, and Clark Kent gets a phone call from them. Superman then puts the kidnappers on hold and calls the B. and W. Cleaners, where his outfit has been misplaced. "Let me describe my suit to you," he says. "The cape is kind of a royal blue with white piping, and the leotards are kind of an off-blue. . . . No, they're not my wife's, no. They're mine. I'm not married. . . . What's that remark supposed to mean? . . . How would you like somebody to leap over tall buildings with a single bound and land on your store? . . . Now this is very difficult to explain. Uh, you see, I sometimes fly in that suit. . . . What do you mean, you bet I do? . . . How would you like somebody to come down there and knock that silly cigar out of your mouth? . . . Never mind how I can see it—I can see it."

Some of the other highlights of *The Windmills Are Weakening* are "Returning the Gift," a monologue about a timid man trying to return a toupee to a department store, and "Ben Franklin in Analysis," a monologue about a psychiatrist who takes on Franklin as a patient. In "Buying a House" Newhart does a scalpel job on real-estate salesmen. According to Newhart, "Realtors are people who didn't make it as used-car salesmen," and in this routine Newhart portrays a realtor who knows no shame in saying absolutely anything to get a sale. "The people who lived here before tell me you can hardly hear anything from the sheet-metal plant across the street," the Newhart character tells some prospective home buyers.

The critic for *Hi-Fi/Stereo Review* wrote that "on the whole this program is brighter and easier to take than other recent discs by this mildly amusing buffoon." And the critic for the *American Record Guide* was even less amused: "Newhart tends to leave many a stone unturned in his search for laughs once he has posited his characters in their promising dilemmas." To anyone who has listened to *The Windmills Are Weakening* recently, these negative comments will seem mystifying, for it is every bit as good as those early Newhart LPs that were so effusively praised by the press.

Newhart's next album, which came out in 1967, was *This Is It!* Unfortunately, *This Is It!* wasn't nearly as enjoyable as *The Windmills Are Weakening,* but there were still a few good moments. In "Prenatal Twins" Newhart tells us that children are much smarter than we give them credit for being. He illustrates this by showing that babies have an intelligence even before birth. Newhart takes on the role of one member of a set of twins who are still residing in the womb. "What time is it anyway?" one twin asks the other. "Three thirty? . . . Morning or afternoon . . . I can never tell the difference. . . . Boy, I got a cramp in my leg that's just driving me crazy. . . . Where the hell does this cord go? Do you know? . . . Maybe we're electric or something. . . . You know what we haven't done in a couple nights that's a lot of fun? Let's press down and give her some false labor pains."

Newhart relates some of his feelings about travel in "On Trains and Planes." He says, "I take trains a lot because I don't like to fly. Now the railroads today are trying to discourage passenger travel, which you may have noticed. They don't want you there and they let you know it. . . . On the trains it's mainly me and a few old guys who tell me how great a President Harding was."

"The most frightening thing to me when I got married," Newhart explains while introducing another routine, "was that there would be one person who knew me better than anybody else. There are dark corners of yourself you don't want anybody to know, but she knows them. For instance, you can fool your friends or your children, even—you can go out to a party and get smashed and they can't tell—but you can't fool your wife." In this bit, entitled "The Daddy of All Hangovers," Newhart portrays a man who's recently returned home after some serious drinking. "Hi, dear. . . . No, I feel fine . . . I'm just sitting here watching television. . . . What? The picture tube's been out for a week, huh? . . . God, I thought I was going blind there for a while. . . . Yes, I know I have your dress on, dear . . . I thought I'd just sit here and in a couple hours I thought I'd try to make it to that chair over there."

During these years Newhart started getting more opportunities to play supporting roles in movies. When Peter Ustinov was casting *Hot Millions,* a 1968 film about an embezzling scheme, he spent weeks looking for an actor "just like Bob Newhart." Finally, Ustinov decided to ask Newhart himself to play the part. *Hot Millions,* which was directed by Eric Till, turned out to be a charmingly entertaining comedy. It's probably the best film that Newhart has appeared in. Ustinov, who also was a co-author of the screenplay, portrays a British criminal intent on stealing millions from an American company—and he accomplishes this heist not with a gun but with a computer. (This is the sort of picture in which crime most definitely does pay.)

Newhart is excellent as William G. Gnatpole, a vice-president of the firm that the Ustinov character swindles. Mr. Gnatpole (an appropriate name) is a stuffy bureaucrat, a typical Organization Man. Not surprisingly, this is the same kind of character that Newhart would play in most of his movies. And it was quite natural that producers would cast him in these roles—not only because he's superb at handling them, but because they're very similar to the characters he has impersonated in his monologues.

Hot Millions did better than expected at the box office, and reviewers had nothing but favorable things to say about it and about Newhart's performance. For instance, Arthur Knight wrote in *Saturday Review* that the film was "utterly absorbing" and that "Bob Newhart is properly acid and officious as [Karl] Malden's fawning assistant."

What is most memorable about *Hot Millions* are the nicely observed touches that make the characters seem much more true to life than what we might expect in a film about a criminal caper. Some of the scenes between Ustinov's character and the Cockney secretary played (wonderfully well) by Maggie Smith manage to be both funny and touching at the same time. Especially good is the moment when she talks him into marrying her; the shyness and reticence of these people are perfectly captured.

Mike Nichols was impressed by Newhart's performance in *Hot Millions,* and asked him to portray Major Major in *Catch-22* (1970). This was Nichols's version of Joseph Heller's famous novel about World War II.

Major Major is a squadron commander with a unique distaste for exercising authority. Attempting to talk to him is an almost surreal experience:

MAJOR MAJOR: Sergeant, from now on I don't want anyone to come in and see me while I'm in my office. Is that clear?

SERGEANT: Yes sir. What do I say to people who want to see you?

MAJOR MAJOR: Tell them I'm in and ask them to wait.

SERGEANT: For how long?

MAJOR MAJOR: Until I've left.

Parts of *Catch-22* are absolutely first-rate and do full justice to Heller's black comedy. And yet the effect of watching the movie is much different from that of reading the book. A movie really needs much more of a clear-cut dramatic structure in order to be effective; *Catch-22* defies filming because it is essentially a series of episodes in which nothing truly develops and in which the characters don't change much. That's part of the point of the book, but it hardly keeps moviegoers on the edges of their seats.

Next, Newhart was cast in *On a Clear Day You Can See Forever* (1970), a musical directed by Vincente Minnelli. The stars of the picture were Barbra Streisand and Yves Montand. Streisand plays Daisy Gamble, an American girl who is hypnotized by a psychiatrist (Montand) and reveals she has been reincarnated many times before. Most of what goes on in the film is pleasant, but the one outstanding element is the marvelous score by Burton Lane. Streisand sings well, of course, and knows how to handle Daisy Gamble, yet she falters in the scenes in which she's supposed to be a nineteenth-century Englishwoman. Streisand's portrayal seems reminiscent of a typical teenage girl's concept of what a "great lady" is like.

Newhart's part in all of this is small, but well realized. He's the president of the college where the psychiatrist teaches, and the Newhart character thoroughly disapproves of the idea of reincarnation, which, he says, "is appalling. It kills ambition, perpetuates human misery, and propagates false hopes. And is obviously a pack of lies."

In 1971 Newhart was in *Cold Turkey,* a comedy about how the residents of a small town are given a chance to win twenty-five million dollars if they can all quit smoking within a month. As Merwin Wren, Newhart is a PR man who convinces Hiram C. Grayson (Edward Everett Horton), the president of a tobacco company, to make this unusual offer.

Cold Turkey was written and directed by Norman Lear and was shot on location in Greenfield, Iowa, a town whose real-life city council voted to ban smoking at the time the picture was being made. The cast was filled with quite a number of well-known comedians, including Dick Van Dyke, Tom Poston, and Bob and Ray.

Cold Turkey got a very mixed reception from movie critics. Roger Greenspun commented in *The New York Times* that the satire "not only is aimed at rather obvious mass attitudes, but also is severely limited by the optimistic attitudes of the same masses." *Newsweek*'s critic said, "The tensions of the town are inflated beyond comic suspension in Lear's attempt to puff up his premise."

Newhart was involved in another film project in 1971, "Thursday's Game," but it wasn't released until three years later. This made-for-television movie was first broadcast April 14, 1974, on ABC. Written and produced by James Brooks, "Thursday's Game" gave Newhart a significantly larger role than in his three previous films.

The story is about two poker-playing buddies (portrayed by

Newhart and Gene Wilder) who continue spending their weekly night out together even after the rest of their friends disband their card group. Harry (Wilder) and Marvin (Newhart) share their problems with each other, and we learn that Marvin's main problem has to do with his wife (played with the right neurotic touch by Cloris Leachman). Says Marvin, "My wife is eight years older than I am. . . . Most people don't know that. They just think she looks bad for her age. . . . How do you leave a woman who makes you feel that guilty? Do you know what she said to me this morning? She said, 'If you ever leave me, I'll kill myself.' And this was just a normal breakfast. We had just finished our juice."

"Thursday's Game" is an amiable, mildly amusing effort, although it seems more like an extended sitcom episode than a real movie. The sentimentality gets to be a bit excessive at times, but most of the performances are appealing enough to keep the viewer watching.

The press had a lot of favorable things to say about this movie. *The New York Times*'s TV critic John J. O'Connor wrote, "'Thursday's Game' . . . happened to be unusually perceptive, marvelously acted, and very funny." And the *Christian Science Monitor* called it "one of the year's best."

In 1970 and 1971 Newhart had made four films. What's more, he was then considering several other movie offers. (And, who knows, if the second "Bob Newhart Show" hadn't become so popular, he might have made a steady career out of working in movie comedies.) As it turned out, though, Newhart wasn't to appear in another one for almost ten years.

7 | CREATING A SITCOM FOR ADULTS

Around the time NBC asked him to star in the first "Bob Newhart Show," the variety series, Newhart had turned down offers from ABC and CBS to do a situation comedy. "That would have been death for me," he told a reporter for *TV Guide* in 1962, "to do the same character week in and week out would have been boring for me and the audiences."

So when David Davis and Lorenzo Music, two producers from Mary Tyler Moore Enterprises, first approached him in 1971 with the idea for the second "Bob Newhart Show," the sitcom, he was hesitant. "I kept saying no," remembers Newhart. "It was kind of a reflex, I guess. Then one day I asked myself why."

David and Music kept after him, and finally won him over. Newhart then told them he had one special request: "I told the creators I didn't want any children, because I didn't want it to be a show about 'how stupid Daddy is, but we love him so much, let's get him out of the trouble he's gotten himself into.'"

In fact, Newhart has such an aversion to children on TV sitcoms that "in the sixth year [of "The Bob Newhart Show"] they wrote a script in which Emily Hartley was pregnant— and I read it," he recalls. "When they called up and asked, 'What do you think of it?' I said, 'I think it's a very funny script. Who are you going to get to play the part of Bob Hartley?'"

Davis and Music, who wrote the pilot episode of the show and who became the executive producers, decided to have Newhart portray a psychologist, Dr. Robert Hartley, who lives in Chicago. "We made him a psychologist," says Music, "because he can bring work home—in this case to his beautiful wife, Suzanne Pleshette. It also supplies us with our basic joke: the psychologist who is a whiz at dealing with other people's frailties, foibles, and hang-ups, but not so hot at dealing with his own."

According to Newhart, "They created the role for me because, after hearing a lot of my material, they decided I'm a good listener, a good reactor to other people's problems, and making me a psychologist is an ideal situation for my type of comedy."

At first, Newhart admits, he had some reservations about portraying a psychologist: "There was always a feeling in this business that shows about psychiatrists are never successful. After all, there's nothing particularly funny about watching a patient in the throes of a seizure, nor are electric shock treatments good for laughs.

"But attitudes toward psychiatry have changed—the image of the fifty-dollars-an-hour-a-visit guy and the couch has changed. Recognizing this, we felt we could be successful by avoiding the serious psychological problems and deal, instead, with lighter phobias like fear of flying." For that reason, Newhart insisted that Dr. Hartley be "a psychologist, not a psychiatrist. Psychiatrists tend to deal with more serious problems."

Newhart remembers that he himself had once had a slight brush with a psychologist before he started appearing on "The Bob Newhart Show." Characteristically, he maintains that he really didn't need to go at all. "What happened was that my wife was going at the time, and I didn't think it was fair to let her go and for me not to. So I went into the office with my feet dragging. I quit after three sessions.

"Actually, I didn't think my hang-ups were that severe. And, too, in comedy you worry that you may change something that will affect your work. You may become so introverted or introspective that you lose your ability to be funny and make people laugh. It has been known to happen with comedians, and I didn't want to take the risk."

He says it was his suggestion that "The Bob Newhart Show" be set in Chicago. "We wanted it set in a big city," he explains, "with all its inconveniences and comedy situations, which the writers can build around. And I'm from Chicago, remember? I still think it's a great city. Only Chicago isn't really a city, it's a state of mind."

As Davis and Music began the task of writing the pilot episode, their intentions were to create a sitcom for adults, something with more subtlety and cleverness than the usual TV fare. They wanted their comedy to be based on characters, not one-liners. "We resisted the temptation to surround Bob with eccentrics," Music told an interviewer for *TV Guide* in 1973. "We favor the identifiable face. We're not trying to do Archie Bunker. We're selling class and charm and wit."

Newhart was fully in agreement with the producers' ideas about the series. "I like the humor to come out of character," he says. "When you're going for a joke, you're stuck out there if it doesn't work. There's nowhere to go. You've done the drum roll and the cymbol clash, and you're out on the end of the plank."

"We see Bob as an actor with great comedy instincts," says Davis. "He will not do jokes. If you try to sneak in a joke, he won't do it. He does attitudes."

While Davis and Music were still writing the pilot, they (and Newhart) were also looking for actors and actresses to play the supporting roles on the show.

Naturally, the most important of these was Bob's leading lady. Without the right chemistry between Newhart and whoever would play Emily Hartley, all of the scriptwriters' terrific ideas would go for nothing.

Davis remembers that he and Music were watching "The Tonight Show" one evening when both Newhart and Suzanne Pleshette were guests. Suzanne read a poem about being in her thirties yet wanting very much to have a baby. "Suzanne started talking," Davis says, "and I looked at Lorenzo and he looked at me. There she was, just what we were looking for. She was revealing her own frailties, talking freely about being over thirty. She was bubbleheaded but smart, loving toward her husband but restless about his imperfections. We were trying to get away from the standard TV wife, and we knew that whoever we picked would have to be offbeat enough and strong enough to carry the show along with Newhart."

Next, "we asked her in for a little chat," remembers Davis, "never believing a movie star like Suzanne would really be interested in our brand of series TV. *Some* chat. Before it was over, we had been talked into one of the craziest deals in the history of television.

"We had agreed that if Suzanne got pregnant while the series was in progress, we would have to write into the scripts the fact that she and Bob were going to have a baby. On the other hand, she promised that she wouldn't start trying to get pregnant until September." (Needless to say, Newhart was hoping that Suzanne's pregnancy would turn out to be timed so as never to be visible on the air.)

Davis says, "We didn't dream Suzanne would accept the part, but after we had negotiated the pregnancy clause, she did. Mostly, I think, because we filmed with three cameras and a live audience one night a week, and she could get home to Tom (her husband, Tom Gallagher) by six o'clock on all the other days."

Suzanne Pleshette says that she was very enthusiastic from the start about the producers' concept of Emily Hartley. "The way it's written, the part *is* me. There's the stream of non sequiturs by which I live. There are fights. I'm allowed to be demonstrative. But the core of the marriage is good. . . . Bob is just like my husband Tommy, letting me go bumbling and stumbling through life."

Before "The Bob Newhart Show," Suzanne Pleshette had had about fifteen years of professional experience as an actress. Though she had never quite become a major box-office attraction, she had received a considerable amount of critical acclaim for her performances in such films as *If It's Tuesday, This Must Be Belgium; Forty Pounds of Trouble; The Birds; Rome Adventure; Nevada Smith;* and *The Geisha Boy.* On Broadway, she had starred in productions of *The Miracle Worker* and *Two for the Seesaw.* In the sixties she played a large number of parts on TV dramas, especially medical shows such as "Ben Casey, "Dr. Kildare," and "Medical Center." "I have suffered every disease known to television playwrights," she says, "and many of the diseases were fatal."

All of this training shows up to good effect on "The Bob Newhart Show," for not only is Suzanne Pleshette a stunning beauty with a sultry voice, she is also a solid actress who seems convincing in almost any situation. She contributes a fiery quality to Emily Hartley that gives the character much more substance than most wives on sitcoms have. Because of her spunk, no one could accuse Emily Hartley of being a doormat; even though Emily loves Bob, it's obvious that he frequently gets on her nerves. And when she does get irritated with him, she's perfectly capable of unleashing a biting wit that makes Bob feel extremely uncomfortable.

For the role of Howard Borden, the Hartleys' next-door neighbor, the producers had Bill Daily in mind all along. Back in the sixties, Daily had become famous for his portrayal of air force pilot Roger Healey in "I Dream of Jeannnie." (His co-stars on that show were Larry Hagman and Barbara Eden.) "We hesitated over having Bill in a uniform again," Davis remembers. "But the idea of a guy working on an airliner, always turned around by the clock, was too good to resist."

Davis says that Daily did a fine job of fleshing out their

concept of Howard Borden. "Bill has caught it all, the whole tone of vulnerability and intensity, the puppy-dog likability, the way he wears his emotions on his sleeve—and he knows how to round it all out in terms of humor."

Daily plays Howard as a guy who's eager and endearingly dopey; his flakiness is in sharp contrast to Bob's rationality. Daily frankly admits loving his role on "The Bob Newhart Show": "It's really a terrific part. More dimensions than a casual viewer might suspect. I can go through fifteen different emotions—and it all plays for me. It's not a big part but it's a total gas. Sometimes in one show I may have only two pages of dialogue. I just run into the next-door apartment, do my gig, and run out again. But the words I get are key words. Crackle words! You better say them right. You can't misplace the rhythm of the words, or the humor flies out the window."

Daily has a wonderful style of delivery, making the most of his lines with his quirky, elliptical, somewhat disjointed way of speaking. Often the words pop out in quick bursts, followed by pauses that Daily uses as masterfully as Newhart himself.

And it's not just a coincidence that Daily pays so much close attention to the rhythms of his delivery, for he was a jazz musician, a bass player, prior to becoming a comedian. He worked at numerous small jazz clubs in Chicago in the early fifties before he even began to think about acting. Later, he began appearing as a comic with an improvisational group in Chicago, and he then became acquainted with another young man trying to break into show business, Bob Newhart.

Newhart recalls that "Bill and I worked very similarly and we'd lend each other material. . . . He was just as funny then as he is now, in the same disarming way."

Daily's memories of growing up in Chicago are radically different from Newhart's, though. "A rough scene, Chicago," Daily says. "I grew up in a rotten neighborhood, very lower middle class. Getting beat up going to school. Always lonely. Music became my only friend." He says that "you've got to be hungry to be a comedian. Ever hear of a rich kid who wanted to be a comic? We want to make people laugh so they'll love us and make up for a bad childhood—that's the story of most comics. Bob Newhart's the only comedian I know who came from a nice home and had a nice childhood. The rest of us? All flipouts, man, all rejects."

The part of Carol Kester on "The Bob Newhart Show" was created especially for Marcia Wallace. Early on, Davis and Music were thinking about having a receptionist in the series, and when they saw Marcia on "The Merv Griffin Show," they decided to write the part to take advantage of the things she does well. "The first day we just wrote her in as a stock character," Music recalls. "But after we heard her read the lines at rehearsal, we rewrote the part. The character is not so much what we created as what she contributes. She gets more laughs than we write in."

Marcia Wallace brings her style of self-deprecating humor to her brightly amusing portrayal of Carol Kester. Admittedly, Marcia's appearance is unusual—she looks a bit like a beanpole with buckteeth—and much of her comedy has to do with her looks. What's more, Carol is not terribly at ease on dates and yet she is almost desperate to land a husband. Marcia confesses to some of the same awkwardness and ambivalent feelings toward the opposite sex. "I can't get used to men lighting my cigarettes," Marcia says. "I always try to light theirs."

Before her fateful appearance on "Merv Griffin," Marcia had been part of the Fourth Wall, an off-Broadway improvisational comedy group, and she had been in some TV commercials and summer-stock productions. Fans of "The Bob Newhart Show" may be surprised to learn that up until just a few years before she got the part of Carol Kester, Marcia Wallace had weighed nearly 230 pounds, almost 100 more than she weighed while she was working on the series. "When I first went to New York," she remembers, "I was incredibly fat, terribly lonely— and selling bedsheets." Not surprisingly, this is just the sort of personal observation that someone like Carol Kester could appreciate and identify with, even though Carol herself was never that heavy.

For the part of Dr. Jerry Robinson, the unorthodox orthodontist who works on the same floor as Dr. Hartley, Davis and Music auditioned over sixty actors. Yet "it was Peter [Bonerz] all the way," according to Music. "The character was designed to be everything Bob Newhart isn't—liberal, wild, volatile. Besides being a very talented performer, Peter happened to *be* Jerry. For example, he can move from one mood to another faster than anyone I know."

Bonerz plays Jerry Robinson as a guy who's very satisfied with himself; if you called Jerry "conceited," he would probably be the first to agree with you. He's a foot-loose bachelor who makes a play for every pretty girl he sees, no matter how foolish he may look if she doesn't respond to him.

Bonerz had appeared, before "The Bob Newhart Show," in several movies, including *Medium Cool, Catch-22* (with Newhart), and *Funnyman*. He says that being cast as Dr. Jerry Robinson was good for his career not just because it made him a familiar face to millions of TV viewers, but because he got a chance to learn a great deal about directing for television. "Being second banana on a series is the perfect opportunity," he explains. "You don't have the strain of carrying the show. You're free to do other things. Ever since I started in film and television, I've put in as much time observing directors as I have acting. It beats waiting around, drinking coffee."

He kept asking the producers for a chance to direct an episode of "The Bob Newhart Show," and when they finally gave him a chance—and when he did the job well—Bonerz became one of the regular directors of the series. (He has since directed episodes of other programs, such as "Mary," starring Mary Tyler Moore.)

With the cast finally set and the first script written, the next step was to shoot the pilot episode. Newhart says he was very pleased with the way things were going at that point. "Dave and Lorenzo did their homework well. . . . They knew my special style of humor when they started out, and they tailored the show around me and the type of comedy I do. We had plenty of time for rehearsals, four days—and if I didn't like the lines in the script, or if it didn't come off sounding like me, the way I'd say it, we'd just change it and work at it until it did sound like me."

The pilot script was entitled "Fly the Unfriendly Skies," and the story was concerned with the fear of flying. In this episode, Bob is the one who's cool and rational about flying, while Emily is afraid to take a plane trip. In real life, however, the roles would be reversed: Newhart is the one with the phobia.

Jack Spatafora, who was a friend of Newhart's in the '50s

and who currently works as a publicist in Chicago, says, "A problem back in the early period for him was that there weren't a lot of clubs in Chicago then, and Bob had a deathly fear of flying, so he wasn't going to do a lot of traveling. . . . For a long time Bob would arrange his engagements so that he could drive or take trains, anything to avoid flying."

Newhart admits, "I'm not that enthusiastic about flying. . . . But I feel safer about flying now, since they've put the plane bars in. And I love the big 747 jumbos. I'd say they're the safest because you've never heard of a hotel lobby crashing, have you?"

At any rate, "Fly the Unfriendly Skies" is quite typical of much of what we would later see on "The Bob Newhart Show." The episode begins with a phone call, handled in the usual Newhart style. Dr. Hartley is saying to one of his patients, "Mrs. Herald, we've been over this before. As you said yourself, you feel that having a beautiful body threatens you. . . . For some reason having a fat body doesn't threaten you. . . . I'm happy to hear you've been able to control it. . . . Mrs. Herald, I'm having trouble understanding you with your mouth full."

Later, Bob tells Emily that he is going to take his fear-of-flying workshop on a flight to New York. And Bob has a surprise for her—an extra ticket for Emily to accompany the group. The news doesn't seem at all agreeable to her, and she is forced to explain to him that she is even more apprehensive about flying than any of his patients:

BOB: You're afraid of flying?

EMILY: That's what I said.

good at it,
w o.ner sit-
condition,
thought, a
laughers."
vrote, "The
y, each con-
w. And one
diosyncrasy.
and his pa-
Bob and his
supporting
that we can

ok, said that
beings, not
. . we grew
s' characters
on, we found
, wondering

opularity was
k has played
walks down
e looks back
much."

. stupid.

in your workshop who are
stupid?

But I don't love *them*.

f his workshop before the
ju have expressed a lack of
ig jets, and that's why I've
a navigator for over fifteen
nillion miles without inci-
eeting—and proceeds, be-
re groups of people larger
anxieties rather than calm-

finally convinces Emily to
rk. She does all right up
bout to take off, but then
e demands that the crew
ff—and they do.
d out very well, and CBS
hat they gave the show an
Mary Tyler Moore Show"
72 prime-time schedule.
elecast on September 16,
clear that the series was
easons the show regularly
in the Nielsen ratings.
rt Show" as much as the
r for *Variety* commented,
omedy in nightclubs be-

fore he ended up on TV. He is not only exceedingly
he also gives distinction to the genre. Like the fe
coms that are willing to touch upon the human
'The Bob Newhart Show' provides some food for
diet not too well served on most of the half-hou

In the *Christian Science Monitor,* Steve Carlson
characters . . . are credible, each having an identit
tributing to the overall comedy effect of the sho
finds a constant interplay between normalcy and i
There are conversations between psychologist Bob
tients. . . . There are little encounters between
strange neighbor (played by Bill Daily). And the
characters include so many recognizable traits
easily identify with their feelings and actions."

Rick Mitz, writing in *The Great TV Sitcom Bo*
"'The Bob Newhart Show' . . . created human
beanbrains, and people who, season after season .
to care about. *Care* about. . . . "Bob Newhart
were so real, so lifelike, that when they weren't c
ourselves thinking about them during the week
how Bob and Emily were doing."

Newhart's reaction to all of this praise and p
typically (and almost absurdly) modest: "Lady lu
a big part in my career. . . . I'm like the guy wh
the street, hears a crash behing him, and when
he sees a safe has fallen and missed him by *that*

Some of the most memorable of Newhart's early TV appearances were on "The Ed Sullivan Show."

Newhart's first movie was *Hell Is for Heroes*, in which he played a meek army headquarters clerk.

In *Hot Millions*, Newhart's character, William G. Gnatpole, is vice president of a firm swindled by the Peter Ustinov character.

For *Catch-22*, Newhart was cast as Major Major, a squadron commander with a unique distaste for exercising authority.

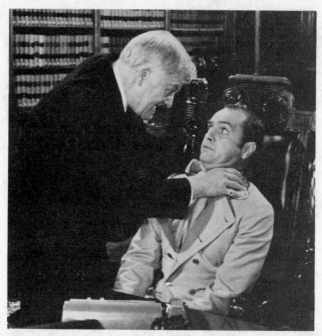

The Reverend Clayton Brooks (Dick Van Dyke) offers some advice to Merwin Wren (Newhart) in *Cold Turkey*.

The characters portrayed by Newhart and Gene Wilder spend a weekly night out together—without their wives—in "Thursday's Game."

The cast of "The Bob Newhart Show" was one of the best ever put together for a sitcom.

In the pilot episode of "The Bob Newhart Show," Emily Hartley (Suzanne Pleshette) reveals to her husband (Newhart) that she's afraid of flying.

Tom Poston played Bob Hartley's buddy Cliff Murdoch, "the Peeper," in several episodes of "The Bob Newhart Show."

Newhart's character takes up long-distance running in "Marathon," a made-for-TV movie.

Sorrowful Jones (Walter Matthau) and Regret (Newhart) discuss what to do with a six-year-old orphan in *Little Miss Marker*.

U.S. President Manfred Link (Newhart) is ineffectual as a chief executive, a father, and a husband in *First Family*.

Dick Loudon, as the host of "Vermont Today," tries to put on a serious, thought-provoking talk show.

Joanna Loudon (Mary Frann) looks on while Dick gives a cheer for his alma mater in a scene from "Newhart."

8 | A CULT FAVORITE— "THE BOB NEWHART SHOW"

One day Emily Hartley comes to Bob's office and interrupts one of his sessions with a patient. She excitedly tells him, "Bob, I just came from the school board and they offered me a full-time job as a kind of administrative adviser. . . . But I told them I couldn't give an answer until I talked to my husband."

Bob is clearly apprehensive, and he tells her that he has his doubts about how this job of hers would affect their marriage. (Previously, she had worked only part-time as a substitute teacher.) Then Bob says, "Now I told you what I think. If you still want to take the job . . . go ahead." And since she very much wants the job, she does take it.

When Emily starts working full-time, though, Bob is soon annoyed that she isn't keeping up with her housework. What's more, she's never in the apartment when he gets home after work. So he gets drunk one evening (with Mr. Carlin, no less, a sure sign that Bob is really desperate) and then later has a talk with Emily:

BOB: I think we have what is called a liberal marriage. We never interfere in each other's important decisions. I would never ask you to do anything that you wouldn't ask me to do. Our marriage is fifty/fifty. I want you to quit.

EMILY: Bob, if I quit my job just because you asked me, then we wouldn't have that fifty/fifty marriage you're talking about.

BOB: Well, how about fifty-one/fifty?

(In the end, however, after she tells him she feels much happier when she works all day, he relents and says it's all right with him if she keeps her job.)

This episode is typical of much of what happens on "The Bob Newhart Show." The marriage of Bob and Emily Hartley seems very true to life: they love each other, yet at the same time there is constant friction between them. The humor of the show is based mainly on the relationship of these two likable characters, and the situations they face are clearly recognizable to all of us.

For instance, in another episode Bob gets a gold watch from Emily for his fortieth birthday. He loves the watch until he discovers how much it cost—$1,300. Bob makes it plain to

Emily that he considers the gift to be wastefully extravagant.
Emily admits the present was a bit lavish, yet she believes that
Bob is being a cheapskate about the whole matter:

EMILY: After all, Bob, I don't do this sort of thing all the
time. . . . Well, if you don't like it, you can just . . .
take it back.

BOB (angrily): No, I can't take it back, because there isn't too
big a demand for watches that say "To Bob, the most
wonderful husband in the world."

EMILY: Well, I'd sure like to rewrite that line.

After fighting over the watch, they go out to a "surprise"
birthday party for Bob, who hates having people make a fuss
over him. When they get back to their apartment, they're
both in an especially irritable mood:

EMILY: Bob, you didn't even try to have a good time.

BOB (standing in front of the bedroom door): Emily, I don't
want to get into that again. . . . I'm exhausted from having such a great time. I'm going to bed—unless you have
another surprise waiting for me.

EMILY: I did have. But you're sure not gonna get it now.

BOB: I didn't expect it.

The scenes in which Bob and Emily have this sort of argu-
ment are often the most entertaining parts of the show. They
needle each other, yet never cut deeply enough for the damage
to be beyond healing. In most TV marriages, on the other
hand, the characters are usually either bellowing at each other
all the time or their relationship is too perfect to be believable.

The characters of Bob and Emily Hartley, though, seem as real as our next-door neighbors.

"The Bob Newhart Show" was consistent not only in popularity, but also in quality—it turned out to be one of the three or four best-written and best-acted sitcoms that have ever been produced. The talented ensemble of performers, which included Suzanne Pleshette, Bill Daily, Marcia Wallace, and Peter Bonerz, worked marvelously together. The writing, which was done by many of the same people who were responsible for "The Mary Tyler Moore Show," assumed a level of intelligence on the part of the viewers. The producers were also very inventive about bringing innumerable changes to the basic setup and never letting the show become stale.

The series was a departure from older sitcoms in many ways. One of the most notable was that Bob and Emily were shown to be carrying on a normal sex life. Many of the best sequences of the series, in fact, are played out in their king-size bed. This extra touch of verisimilitude adds quite a bit to the realism of Bob and Emily's relationship. (In the fifties and sixties sitcoms, it must be remembered, TV wives and husbands always slept in twin beds. So these scenes in the Hartley bedroom, which seem very tame today, were actually almost avant-garde in 1972.) The scripts of "The Bob Newhart Show" often make it obvious that Bob and Emily enjoy sleeping together. For example, at the end of the pilot episode, Bob Hartley and Jerry Robinson are talking together after Bob has returned from his trip to New York with his fear-of-flying workshop. Jerry hears that Bob has received a stack of congratulatory messages, including one from Emily telling Bob he was "sensational":

JERRY: I didn't think Emily went with you to New York.

BOB: No, she didn't. She's referring to something that happened this morning.

When asked by a reporter in August 1972 to describe Bob and Emily's relationship, Suzanne Pleshette replied, "They hug, kiss, go to bed, laugh, fight, and that's what life's about. Yes, they sleep in the same room in the same bed."

We do get a clear sense from watching the series that Bob and Emily are well matched. Their personalities complement each other nicely: Bob is quiet and phlegmatic, while Emily is more spirited and excitable. Of course, these same differences that must have attracted them to each other initially are also the cause of most of the friction between them.

Robert Hartley is a fairly successful psychologist who lives with his wife Emily in a condominium apartment on Lake Shore Drive in Chicago. He's an amiable, well-meaning sort of guy who treats everyone with consideration. Sometimes he's even a bit too kindhearted for his own good, though, and people try to take advantage of him. When Carol Kester, Bob's receptionist, reminds him on one occasion about a patient who hadn't paid a bill from the year before, he replies, "Oh, she'll pay eventually." (Carol then says to Jerry, "You see we're trying to straighten out the affairs of Robert Hartley, Inc., a nonprofit organization.")

Even though he talks to many people as a psychologist (or maybe because of this), Bob is not usually a gregarious person. Instead, he prefers to stick to a small circle of friends he is comfortable with. When Emily wants to invite two teachers from her school over for dinner, she tells him, "I didn't think it would hurt to meet two new people." His response to this is "I know enough people already."

Bob is not as articulate about his feelings for Emily as she would like him to be. "Do you love me?" she asks him on one occasion. He replies, "Sure, why not?"

Emily often wishes that he could be more straightforward and direct about saying what he thinks. For instance, they have this exchange in one episode in which Emily accompanies Bob to one of his group sessions with his patients:

EMILY: Bob, you never told me not to come up here.

BOB: I said, "Do you really want to come up here?"

EMILY: You call *that* telling me?

BOB: It's my way of telling you.

EMILY: Well, Bob, the next time you don't want me to do something, don't ask me, just tell me.

BOB: Do you really think there'll be a next time?

EMILY: What are you trying to say?

BOB: You figure it out.

Newhart's performance as Bob Hartley is often a true delight, wonderfully understated and handled in an easy-does-it style. Newhart's rapid eye blinks, which he uses when Bob Hartley is feeling disconcerted or irritated, are his comic trademark, much like Groucho's cigar or Chaplin's baggy pants.

Newhart gets to do his funniest reactions on those occasions when his character is feeling the greatest amount of embarrassment. One of the most entertaining shows of the series is the episode in which Emily learns that Bob had been dating an-

other girl, Gloria Webster, at the same time he had been dating her. (In fact, he only broke up with Gloria the week before
he married Emily.) Bob is clearly mortified as he stammers
(and tries, ineffectually, to smile) his way through this sequence, while Emily becomes increasingly exasperated.

EMILY: Is that true, Bob? Were you going out with Gloria at
the same time you were going out with me?

BOB: Not exactly. It was sort of like . . . uh, changing the
guard.

EMILY: You want to explain that?

BOB: Yeah, I guess I better. You see, when the new guard
comes out, the old guard leaves. And for a moment or
two there, they're kind of both there together, you
know. . . . How's that?

About Newhart's acting on the series, Suzanne Pleshette
comments, "I always thought of him as a great comedian, and
he's become a fine actor and is totally responsible for the
humor on the show. Newhart is a hip man, much more exciting than the Hartley character he plays.

"It's too bad the scripts so seldom require him to laugh or
smile—Bob has a fabulous smile that truly lights up his face.
But he's low-key, and that's a trait some people mistake for
weakness. This is not true of Bob. His compassion and his
reason are responsible for his strength."

She also says that Newhart "had to learn that by nature I'm
a hugger, a toucher, and it took him quite a while to become
comfortable with that sort of thing. He isn't demonstrative. . . . Sometimes when we kissed on the show, he

didn't connect at all—he sort of kissed the air. It's the only time you can believe he was once an accountant."

As a psychologist, Bob Hartley's methods are as low-keyed as Newhart is himself. Dr. Hartley's patients never make any dramatic "breakthroughs"; in fact, says Newhart, "He never cured anyone . . . never had one successful case that he could point to." Instead of primal screams or electric shock, his patients just slowly inch their way toward becoming slightly less neurotic.

Once, a hard-hitting woman TV interviewer tries to get him to admit, on the air, that he never solves anyone's problems. Dr. Hartley cringes a lot, but still tries to defend himself in this scene:

INTERVIEWER: You mean you ask forty dollars an hour and you guarantee nothing?

BOB: Well, I validate.

INTERVIEWER: Is that your answer? . . . Do you ever cure anybody?

BOB: Well, I wouldn't say "cure."

INTERVIEWER: So your answer is no.

BOB: No, my answer is not no. I get results.

Bob feels that his methods, however slow, are humane, and he puts a high value on treating his patients with respect. He always tries to put them at ease. Most of what Bob says in his office consists of reassuring platitudes. When a patient who's been seeing UFOs asks if he's "ready for the loony bin," Dr. Hartley replies, "We try to shy away from words like *crazy* and *loony bin.*"

Viewers are introduced to quite a number of Bob's regular patients over the course of six years' worth of episodes. There's meek Mr. Peterson, who makes even Dr. Hartley look like a raging bull. There's lonely Michele Nardo, who's always having trouble getting a date.

But the most interesting patient—and the most disturbed—is definitely Mr. Elliot Carlin (adeptly played by Jack Riley), a bitter, nasty man who has a persecution complex. He seems to feel a sense of hostility toward everyone and everything around him. He also suffers from a lack of self-esteem, a total disregard for the feelings of others, and a long list of other problems. Mr. Carlin's main role on the series is to stick a pin into Dr. Hartley's platitudes about thinking positive and becoming happier.

In one episode, Mr. Carlin begs Carol Kester to go out with him, and when she agrees, he says, "I'm beginning to lose respect for you already."

Before his date with her, Mr. Carlin is plainly very nervous. To bolster his confidence, Bob tells him, "Just be natural, just be yourself." To which Mr. Carlin responds, "It's hard to be natural when you're wearing a toupee, contact lenses, and four-inch lifts."

On another occasion, Mr. Carlin says, "I was all alone on my last birthday, except for my pet hamster—and I *own* him."

Emily Hartley, a teacher at the Tracy Grammar School, is (in the sharpest possible contrast to Mr. Carlin) warm, witty, and considerate. "Emily is not smarter than Bob," explains Suzanne Pleshette, "nor is she manipulative like most wives in television series. She is appreciative of Bob's idiosyncrasies, and he respects her desire for an identity of her own." Emily can needle Bob, and yet all the while convey the sense of still loving him and being devoted to him.

During the course of "The Bob Newhart Show," the character of Emily Hartley changed somewhat, just as a real person would during six years. In the early episodes she seems more content to be a housewife, working only part-time as a substitute teacher. Later, she spends much more of her time teaching and becomes increasingly involved with her work. (She's eventually made vice principal at her school.) It is made clear that she's an excellent teacher and that her students are very loyal to her.

There are several key episodes in which we can see Emily becoming more assertive than she was early on. In one, Emily attends Bob's consciousness-raising group, and the other women convince her to change her perspective a bit concerning her own marriage. She tells Bob, "There are lots of things that I want to do that I don't do because you don't want to."

In another episode, Emily is pressured by the principal of her school to skip a bright student, Richard Lewis, from third grade to fifth grade; the boy's father is on the school board and is determined to have his son advanced. But Emily thinks that the boy isn't emotionally ready for fifth grade, and she is willing to fight with her superiors over this issue. "The minute somebody pushes me, my impulse is to push back," she says to Bob.

At times, Emily can be something of a complainer and a worrier, but despite these faults, she is basically a well-balanced person. Part of Emily and Bob's function on the show is for them to play the part of normal, sensible people, in contrast to some of the more eccentric characters, such as Howard Borden or Elliot Carlin.

The Hartleys' next-door neighbor, Howard Borden, who works as an airplane navigator, is a gentle, sweet-tempered fellow. He's engaging, but at the same time not terribly brainy. In fact, he seems to misunderstand most of what goes on around him. Part of the joke about the character is that we wonder how he manages to navigate a Boeing 747 when he can scarcely navigate himself from one room to another.

For instance, when Howard learns that Emily has joined a consciousness-raising group, he says, "That sounds like a worthy cause. I hope you raise a lot."

Howard does some peculiar things. Once he tells Bob, "I need insurance. I can't keep putting money into those little machines at the airport. The passengers are starting to look at me funny."

The Hartleys never have any children (as Newhart insisted), but Howard seems to look at Bob and Emily as if they were his parents. He's always coming over to visit, he eats most of his meals with them, and he's in the habit of borrowing everything he needs from their apartment. He even gets Emily to do his sewing for him. Howard is totally devoted to Bob and Emily, and he probably would rather allow one of his planes to crash than do something they disapproved of.

Howard was once married (he has a son, Howie, who lives with his ex-wife, Lois), and comes close at one point in the series to marrying Bob's sister Ellen. Howard is infatuated with Ellen from the time they first meet, yet she always has her doubts about how their marriage would work out. After all, being married to someone like Howard Borden would be like being married to a child. He's very nice, but too much sweetness would be hard for any woman to take for very long.

Carol Kester, the receptionist on Bob's floor, has a habit of putting herself down at every opportunity. Once she makes a phone call for Bob and then tells him, "It really bugs me to talk to a machine that has a better personality than I have." A typical remark from Carol is often something like this: "I took a gourmet cooking class and I know how to fix this dish for six people. Now if I only knew six people. . . ."

She is given most of the wisecracks on "The Bob Newhart Show," because it fits her personality for her to be making clever, often self-deprecating, remarks. She frequently makes fun of the importance (or lack thereof) of her job. When Emily tells Carol about the dilemma she's facing with one of her elementary students, Carol replies, "I don't see anything wrong with skipping a grade—because I skipped myself and it turned out great. Here I am, an incredibly successful receptionist. I've hit my professional peak and I'm only thirty years old."

Carol is unashamedly man-hungry. She frankly admits to lusting after quite a number of eligible men. When she meets Ruth Corley, a Chicago talk-show host, they have this exchange:

CAROL: I loved that show you did with Robert Redford and George Segal.

RUTH: Believe me, they're just ordinary guys. They put their pants on one leg at a time.

CAROL: Yeah, I'd just love to be there and watch.

In a later episode of the show, Carol finally does get married, though—to Larry Bondurant. Yet this move was probably not a wise one on the scriptwriters' part, for the Carol

Kester character is essentially, like Rhoda Morgenstern from "The Mary Tyler Moore Show," forever single.

Dr. Jerry Robinson is an orthodontist who works in an office down the hall from Dr. Hartley's. Jerry has a reputation of being quite a ladies' man, and we are introduced to many different women that he goes out with. The most stunning of all of these (and the most intelligent) is Courtney Simpson. She's a long-legged beauty and she works as a marine biologist. Jerry is so smitten by her that he goes with Courtney to Tahiti for a whole month. While under her spell, he says strange things like this: "Bob, this is the real me, the new me, the free me that I used to be before I became the old me."

Most of the time, though, Jerry's interest in women rarely gets beyond their physical charms. For instance, in one episode we see him trying to seduce a Swedish girl who doesn't understand English.

Jerry is extremely self-centered; he becomes concerned about other people's feelings only in the event of a real emergency. Any fan of "The Bob Newhart Show" is aware that one would not describe Jerry as "sensitive." When Bob and Jerry try on one occasion to comfort Howard, who's afraid he's losing Ellen, Jerry says, "Worrying's not going to help, Howard. If Ellen really goes for that kind of guy, you've lost her anyway. . . . What I mean is, if that guy were really that fantastic, she would've married him in the first place. So he can't be that appealing. . . . Of course, Ellen's no queen of the hop, either. She's been around the block a couple of times. Her doors aren't exactly crashing down from guys trying to get to her." As he leaves the room, Jerry tells Howard and Bob, both of whom are incensed at him by this point, "Glad I could help."

Since the series was doing so well in the ratings, it came as a real surprise when Newhart announced in January 1977 that he planned to end the show after the fifth season was completed. He said he was concerned that there might be a dropping off in the quality of the scripts if the show continued for too long. "I didn't want to limp off the air with a show that didn't measure up to what it had been a few years earlier," he explained. Newhart also said he was tired of the weekly grind of a series and wanted to do more films and concerts.

The executives at Mary Tyler Moore Enterprises and at CBS weren't the only ones who were disappointed that he was intending to leave. "You wouldn't believe the number of people who bothered to sit down and write," Newhart recalls. "People who said, 'Thank you for giving us so many good times,' and things like that."

So he changed his mind about ending the series after the fifth season. "Both MTM and CBS were so darned nice to me, I got to thinking: 'Why not go ahead another year? What's so tough about it?' People were already starting to say I was quitting because I wouldn't have Mary ("The Mary Tyler Moore Show") anymore as a lead-in, which was nonsense."

After the sixth season, though, Newhart finally did call it quits; the last episode of "The Bob Newhart Show" was broadcast on August 26, 1978. Still, Newhart admits to having had second thoughts about his decision right up until the end. After he told CBS executives he was going to leave, "The next thing I knew we were having a wrap party and it was all over. I'm not sure I meant them to take me that seriously."

He remembers that "the night of the wrap party somebody told me they were tearing down the set and why didn't I go and pick up a souvenir? I couldn't. I couldn't bear watching them tear it down."

The final episode, the one hundred twentieth of the series, was entitled "Happy Trails to You." In it, we learn that Bob has accepted a teaching job at a small college in Oregon. His patients from Chicago are, of course, all distressed at the news. Jerry tells Bob, "When those people first came to you they were hopeless neurotics. Ah, but now they've become hopeless neurotics with a place to go."

Before they leave town, Emily has a suggestion for Bob. "You know what would be nice?" she says to him. "If we would tell our friends how we really feel about them." "Fine," Bob replies. "Why don't *you* do it." By the end of the episode, however, Bob does manage to let everyone know how much he'll miss them when he and Emily move to Oregon.

Up until the time when they made this final episode, says Newhart, "We hadn't slipped in any way. The show was still funny, which is the time to get off. But I felt like a club fighter, the way the other networks threw everything at us. I was very proud of our show but chagrined that the show and the people on it were never truly acknowledged by the TV industry: not one Emmy. We had so many good people— Suzanne Pleshette, Bill Daily, Marcia Wallace, Peter Bonerz, and the rest, and they all made it look too easy."

It does seem astonishing that "The Bob Newhart Show" never picked up an Emmy. During the seventies, "The Mary Tyler Moore Show" and "All in the Family" were the series that were given most of the awards for situation comedies.

While "Mary Tyler Moore" certainly deserved its high reputation, "All in the Family" seems pretty dated today, and it was clearly a mistake for the Emmy-award voters to overlook Newhart's sitcom. On the other hand, the reason that "The Bob Newhart Show" wasn't honored with an award isn't particularly difficult to figure out: the show, like Newhart himself, is quiet and understated and tends to go about its business of being consistently entertaining in a dependable, unspectacular way.

After the last episode of "The Bob Newhart Show" was shown on CBS, the series immediately went into syndication, where it has developed an intensely loyal cult following during the past few years. A story in *The New York Times* in 1982 reported, "Newhart's shows have become such a favorite with [college] audiences that they have spawned a particular brand of cultish behavior: when groups of students watch reruns of 'The Bob Newhart Show,' they pass around a can of beer, and each time Dr. Hartley is referred to as 'Bob' the student who has the beer must take a swallow. When a character says 'Hi, Bob' the student who has the beer must empty the can. 'I am responsible,' said Mr. Newhart, shaking his head, 'for hangovers all over this country.'" Newhart may not be thrilled with what these fans of his are doing, but he must take pleasure in the thought that "The Bob Newhart Show" was so amusing and well-crafted a series that audiences are continuing, years later, to follow the reruns with such enthusiasm.

9 | CRITICAL SUCCESSES, BOX-OFFICE FIASCOES

Without a series to do each week, Newhart made a point of taking things fairly easy for the next few years. He spent a lot of time playing golf—though he eventually gave it up for several years because "I was down to an eight handicap and figured it was as good as I was going to get."

"I can afford to be independent," he told a reporter for the New York *Daily News* in 1980. "My TV series put me in a nice financial position, since I owned a piece of it. So if I didn't work for another three weeks, I wouldn't be hurting." That is a typical Newhart understatement, of course: he probably could have afforded to have taken the next three decades off.

Unlike many other comedians who are often so obsessed and driven by their need to work that they are unable to relax and enjoy themselves, Newhart seems to be a well-adjusted individual who loves to work, but who relishes his leisure time as well. And the success of "The Bob Newhart Show" gave him the freedom to do whatever he wanted to do.

He invested his money wisely and has avoided falling into the traps that so many other celebrities have fallen into. He's a devoted family man and has managed to keep his name completely absent from the gossip magazines. (The idea of hearing some rumor about Newhart that bordered on the scandalous, or even the mildly dishonorable, is hard to imagine.) Essentially, Newhart is a very private person who feels most comfortable with a small circle of friends that he's known for years—people like Dick and Dolly Martin and Don and Barbara Rickles. (Says Newhart, "*Somebody* has got to be Don's friend.")

The place where Newhart did most of his relaxing and socializing during the years between his sitcoms was his beautiful home in Bel-Air, California. He moved there in 1975 and has lived there ever since. He remembers that "one day we were driving on an unfamiliar road and suddenly Ginny yelled, 'Stop the car!' I thought we must have hit somebody's cat or something. I slammed on the brakes, and Ginny said, 'There's the dream house I've always wanted.'" A few months later, the house was theirs.

Set on a hillside, the Newharts' Britanny-style home with its gabled roof and leaded windowpanes has a certain fairy-tale quality about it. When Don Rickles first saw the house, he remarked, "Where are the dwarfs? And where's Snow White?" Guests at the Newhart house may have trouble finding any dwarfs, but they will probably spot a sign outside that says "Armed Dog." "I had it made to order at a hardware store," explains Newhart. "You'd be amazed how many people don't even notice it. I mean, around here they're so conditioned to signs like 'Attack Dog' and 'Armed Guard On Duty.' I just put the two together."

Inside the house, everything is kept very neat and in near-perfect order. "I guess there's a stability that we all require," Newhart says, "because so much of a comedian's early life is spent in motel rooms, working clubs. Also, when I was growing up near Chicago, we never lived in a house, just apartments, so a home is really important to me."

He does keep a number of things around, though, to remind him of his early years in Chicago: "I insisted on buying a big rolltop desk, because during high school I worked at an insurance company where they had row upon row of rolltop desks, and now whenever I don't feel like sitting down and writing a new routine, I look at that desk and think, 'You could still be back there.'"

Personal memorabilia are kept all over the house. His Peabody Award, two Gold Records, three Grammys, and the "Sword of Loyola" award from his alma mater hang in his den—along with a personal letter from President John F. Kennedy and a lithograph by Senator Edward Kennedy (Newhart has frequently worked for the Kennedy political campaigns).

Also ubiquitous around the house are television sets. "There are three in the kitchen alone," explains Newhart, who is an obsessive sports watcher, "and two in Ginny's dressing room, one in mine, one in the cabana . . . at least sixteen altogether."

Besides sports, Newhart takes a strong interest in collecting art, especially archaeological objects from the pre-Christian era. "My favorite acquisition was a Greek vase for bath oils or something. It was real old, but it was in incredible condition. I just loved to touch it." Unfortunately, his children also loved to touch the vase—which soon became history. "It was something that had lasted over two thousand years, then it came into our house and lasted maybe two."

Ginny Newhart, on the other hand, has made a point of collecting vintage models of telephones, the object with which her husband has been so closely associated during his career. His attitude toward telephones is quite different, however. "I hate the telephone," he explains. "I let it ring until Ginny gets it. I don't think it's a phobia—I'm just not a phoner."

The Newharts hired interior designer Phyllis Rowen Sugarman to decorate their home, though she recalls that she often encountered strong resistance from Bob, who has lots of very definite personal preferences. "The one type of decor I can't live with is Chinese," Newhart says, "although I love French. One day I came home and found this Chinese fabric on the living room couches. Everyone kept telling me it was 'chinoiserie'—a French word for an Oriental look. I thought the best thing to do was to have our Chinese laundry man come in and see if he recognized it. For a long time I've had the feeling that I'm the only sane person in the world, anyway. All of my humor is based on that. So when I run into these situations where I think it's Chinese and people tell me it's French I'm conditioned to accept it."

Phyllis Sugarman says that "the house is as delightfully low-key as Bob himself, and that quality is, of course, what makes him the most enduring comedian on TV."

It was after the Newharts moved to their current home that they had their fourth child, Courtney, born in 1978. "When we had just three children," remembers Newhart, "I used to talk with my wife about how nice it would be to get an apartment and travel when the kids were grown and out of school. . . . We had it all worked out and then Ginny got pregnant again. Her first reaction on learning the news in the doctor's office was 'Oh, my God! Bob will be seventy when the baby graduates from college.' That's true enough, but Courtney keeps me young these days. It's great to go home every night and see the little kid. I can't imagine what life would be without her."

In recent years Newhart has been performing his stand-up routines much less frequently than he did in the sixties. Still, he gave a show at the White House a few years ago in which he entertained all fifty United States governors. "I asked them, 'It's ten p.m.—do you know where your lieutenant governor is?'"

Besides the occasional concert or TV guest spot, Newhart's professional activities during the period between his two sitcoms were confined mainly to three movies, "Marathon" (1980), *Little Miss Marker* (1980), and *First Family* (also released in 1980). All of these movies received a number of favorable notices from the critics, especially *First Family,* but none of them proved to be popular with audiences. Newhart goes so far as to call the films "eminently unsuccessful."

"Marathon," directed by Jackie Cooper, is a mildly amusing made-for-TV film in which Newhart portrays a married, middle-aged cost accountant who falls for a shapely stewardess half his age who's played by Leigh Taylor-Young. The story, it must be admitted, is a bit on the predictable side. (Newhart's character, named Walter, is tempted—as any man would be—to have an affair with the girl, but in the end he returns to his wife, Anita.) Still, we are treated to several funny sequences along the way.

At the beginning Walter is about to start running the New York Marathon. We are shown some nicely photographed views of the race (taken by cameramen during the running of the 1979 New York Marathon). Walter tells us, "On a cold gray October morning in New York, 11,533 obsessed souls got together to run a marathon. I was one of them. And my question is Why? I mean, after all, the first guy to do a marathon was a messenger, and you know what happened to him. He ran 26 miles, delivered the message that the Spartans had won the Battle of Marathon, and dropped dead. So here I am running the same 26 miles, and I don't even have any news." The reason, we soon learn, that Walter, who lives in Los Angeles, is running the marathon in New York is that the stewardess has coaxed him into trying it. He seems to have a lot of trouble saying "no" to anything she asks him to do.

One of Newhart's best moments in "Marathon" comes when we see, in a flashback, how he first met the girl, whose name is Barrie. At a ten-kilometer race in California, Walter spots her and is immediately smitten by her. To impress Barrie, Walter tries to act as if he's a first-class long-distance runner. He attempts to run along at the same pace that she's going at. But to his embarrassment, he can't keep up and soon falls behind—utterly exhausted. It turns out that she is not only beautiful, but also a terrific athlete.

Later, Walter enrolls in a yoga class with Barrie. There's an amusing sequence in which Walter keeps eyeing the girl while endeavoring to do the (extraordinarily difficult) exercises. When she notices him looking at her, he hurriedly takes off his wedding ring—only to drop it and have it roll across the floor.

Jerry Krupnick, a syndicated TV critic, wrote in his column that "Newhart is an absolute gem in this story of a quiet, mousy kind of guy whose only vice up to his almost fiftieth year has been his passion for running. . . . Newhart continually proves he can endure better than any other comedian in the business."

Some of the other performers do a credible job in the picture, but most of the laughs in "Marathon" come from Newhart's reactions. It's the one film of Newhart's that could almost have been an episode of one of his sitcoms. Unfortunately, the ratings for "Marathon," which was first shown on CBS on January 20, 1980, weren't high enough to make producers eager to cast him in more movies for television.

Walter Matthau is the center of attention in *Little Miss Marker*. He scowls his way through most of his scenes, playing an unsmiling tightwad named Sorrowful Jones. With a voice that has all of the sweet tones of a bandsaw cutting wood and a face that has the seediest features since W. C. Fields, Matthau often manages to be irresistibly funny. Regrettably, though, the movie begins well, but tends to soften into sentimentality later on.

The story of *Little Miss Marker,* directed by veteran scriptwriter Walter Bernstein, concerns a bookmaker (Matthau) who accepts a six-year-old-girl (played by Sara Stimson) as a "marker" from a gambler who owes him money. The gambler dies, leaving the girl an orphan, and Sorrowful Jones winds up having to look after her.

Newhart plays Sorrowful Jones's droll assistant, Regret, who's bewildered by most of what his boss decides to do. When Jones wants to defy a gangster (portrayed by Tony Curtis), Regret reminds him of certain facts:

SORROWFUL JONES: The last time he bothered me I threw him in the river.

REGRET: The last time he bothered you, he was twelve years old and hadn't killed anyone yet.

The movie is based on a Damon Runyon story, and most of the underworld characters speak in a colorful style that is familiar from other Damon Runyon works, such as *Guys and Dolls*. At one point, for instance, Regret tells Sorrowful Jones, "I have even been told that there are certain jockeys who cannot be fixed at all, but if you ask me, I have always considered that a fairy tale for people who believe in fairies."

Towards the latter part of the film, Sorrowful Jones falls for Amanda Worthington (Julie Andrews), a society lady with an enthusiasm for horse racing. (She owns a horse, Sir Gallahad, so slow that, according to Sorrowful Jones, "it would only win if it was the only horse in the race—and then it would have to come from behind.")

Little Miss Marker includes a number of effective gags. When Sir Gallahad runs, Sorrowful Jones pays off all the other jockeys to throw the race. But Sir Gallahad is so poor a runner that the other jockeys have their hands full in managing to lose. In another scene the little girl asks Jones to read her a bedtime story. Grudgingly, he picks up a newspaper—and then proceeds to read her an account of a horse race.

Sara Stimson was selected by Jennings Lang, the producer of *Little Miss Marker,* out of thousands of five-, six-, and seven-year-old girls who auditioned for the part. (By the way, the character is never referred to by name; she is always just called "the kid.") Lang says, "We definitely decided that we wanted a nonactress. There's less of a gamble in the child who's never performed before. They haven't had a chance to take on any bad habits. It was painful to watch some of the little girls in their Shirley Temple wigs. Their eyes looked as though they expected their mothers to whip them."

Many of the reviewers had positive things to say about both *Little Miss Marker* and Newhart's performance. For example, John Skow, writing in *Time,* commented that "everything is first-class. . . . The supporting cast, including Bob Newhart, Julie Andrews, and Brian Dennehy, is fine too." The *Hollywood Reporter* said, "Matthau, who also executive produced, seems born to play a Runyon character and his performance here is magnificent. . . . The story is still an entertaining one. . . . Bob Newhart is fine as Matthau's sidekick."

For his next picture, Newhart chose to appear in *First Family,* which was written and directed by Buck Henry. Newhart recalls, "When I first saw the script of the movie *First Family,* I was bowled over. It was hilarious. It couldn't miss. . . . As it turned out, I don't think it ever showed in theaters. They put it on airplanes the first night. But if I were to see a script like that again, I'd do it."

First Family is a satirical farce about a U.S. president named Manfred Link (played by Newhart) who does an extremely ineffectual job of managing his administration and conducting his foreign policy. The story concerns the efforts of the Link administration to get Upper Gorm, a small African country, to side with America in an important vote in the United Nations. *First Family* is an especially uneven film—some scenes are very clever, while others fall totally flat. It's similar in many ways to the sketches on NBC's "Saturday Night Live" (and, after all, not only Buck Henry, but some of the members of the cast of *First Family* have appeared on "Saturday Night Live").

The movie was highly praised by several critics. In his review for *The New York Times,* Vincent Canby wrote, *"First Family* . . . features the finest collection of comedy performances to be seen in any one movie this year. . . . Mr. Newhart plays President Link in his matchless button-down manner, doing his best to appear unflappable even when all is lost. Miss [Madeline] Kahn is a constant delight as his wife. . . . Mr. [Harvey] Korman (who plays a U.S. ambassador) is nothing less than one of the greatest sketch actors in the English-speaking world."

Jack Kroll, reviewing the film for *Newsweek,* said that "Newhart is inspired casting: his low-voltage style is perfect for a president of affable vacuity whose chief policy is to prevent his randy 28-year-old daughter from losing her virginity while he's in office."

Gilda Radner portrays President Link's sex-starved daughter; she tries to escape from the watchful eyes of the Secret Service men by tying bed sheets into a rope and climbing down from her White House bedroom. Richard Benjamin is an administration press secretary who tells reporters, "We didn't cancel this morning's press conference. We just didn't have it." Bob Dishy plays a meek vice-president who's hurt that no one takes him seriously. At one point he tries to speak up at a meeting of advisers, only to have President Link say, "Does anyone want to hear what a vice-president thinks?"

Buck Henry clearly aims to make fun of the way that politicians abuse the English language. Here's a sample excerpt from one of President Link's speeches: "And so, my fellow Americans, allow me in closing to emphasize once again that the aims and purposes of this administration are the aims and purposes of all other citizens, men, women, and children, regardless of sex, regardless of color—black, white, red, yellow, and all of the equally attractive shades in between."

One of the funniest bits in the movie is the sequence in which President Link tells one of his aides about the mysterious dream he's been having over and over: "When I was your age, I used to have big dreams. I'd hit a home run with three men on. I'd discover boxes filled with rubies, mow down Nazi troops, bang movie stars. Once I protected a blind newspaper boy from six giant hoods, just with my quick fists and my bare wits. Those were the nights. . . . But now I dream about being in the White House dining room, and I sit down. In front of me there's a bowl of clear soup. Bouillon. And I pick up my soup spoon, and I eat my clear soup. And that's it. . . . Have you ever heard of a dream that didn't mean anything?"

The best reason to see *First Family* is to watch some of the excellent comic performances by Newhart, Benjamin, Dishy, Kahn, Korman, Radner, Austin Pendleton, and Rip Torn. On the other hand, even these talented people can't do much with some of the jokes that misfire. The script often relies on using obscenities for shock value to add some easy laughs to scenes that would otherwise bomb completely. Other gags are drawn out and milked for much more than they're worth, such as a sequence in which we are repeatedly shown that the Americans and the Upper Gormese can't understand each other's language.

Newhart says that when he worked on the film, he was "playing the role without a particular president in mind. It's really four presidents rolled into one. There's the pettiness of Richard Nixon, the use of power of Lyndon Johnson, the humanity of Gerald Ford, and the folksiness of Jimmy Carter. But by and large, my character is a president who is totally unprepared for the enormity of the office, as I'm sure all presidents are." He adds, "I think any president is in a certain sense an extraordinary man. He must have intellectual ability, blind ambition, drive, power, or whatever you want to call it. The demands put upon a president are enormous, and audiences will see me visually aging in the picture."

Newhart explains that he was quite careful in choosing his movie roles. "After the TV series, I didn't want to play anything that even resembled Bob Hartley. . . . Naturally, I wasn't looking for a Hamlet-type role, just something removed from what viewers had seen of me for years. In *Little Miss Marker* I play a Runyonesque-type character, and in [*First Family*] I'm about as far away from Bob Hartley as you can get."

First Family is the most recent movie in which Newhart has appeared, and it will probably be the last one for several years to come—at least so long as his current sitcom stays on the air. Even though Newhart did a fine job in many of his performances, he has never achieved that much recognition as a movie actor. He's never had a "breakthrough" film. Part of the reason for this surely has to do with luck and timing, but part of the reason may also be that Newhart's genial, low-key presence is more suited to television than to the big screen.

10

"I'M ASKING FOR LIGHTNING TO STRIKE TWICE"

During those years when Newhart was away from the routine of appearing in a weekly series, he was disappointed at the quality of most of what he saw on TV. "I thought I was finished," he remembers. "Even dramatic shows were exemplified by kid stuff like 'Wonder Woman.' I thought to myself that with this kind of junk aimed at the twelve-year-old audience, how could there be a place for me? . . . I did an occasional movie, but I missed the immediate reaction of a live studio audience.

"From time to time Bud Grant, the head honcho at CBS, would send over scripts for pilots for me, but they were all clones of what had been successful the season before. When 'Mork and Mindy' was a success for one season, I expected a script in which I would be the father of an extraterrestrial visiting the earth. I kept sending back polite 'no's.'"

But by 1981 Newhart felt that things were beginning to change. "There were two shows that weren't too successful, but at least they made some adult sense. They were 'The Two of Us,' with Peter Cooke and Mimi Kennedy, and 'House Calls,' with Wayne Rogers and Lynn Redgrave. I said, 'Aha, maybe grown-up things are coming back.' So I called my manager, Arthur Price, and I said, 'I think I want to go back to series TV.'

"Price then called Bud Grant and said, 'I'm not promising you anything, but I just *may* be able to talk Bob Newhart into doing another series.' Here I was, hot to trot, and Arthur is talking as if it's a long shot, but he might be able to persuade me. CBS took the bait, with Arthur insisting that I get a good time slot, a lot of money, and good writers."

Next, Newhart had to come up with an idea for the new series. (For most actors or producers, it's an enormous job to convince network executives to buy a new TV series; Newhart, on the other hand, could probably scribble a note on a 3-by-5 card and have the networks ready to commit themselves to the first thirteen episodes.) He was aware that many of his most loyal fans still felt a special affection for Suzanne Pleshette, Peter Bonerz, Bill Daily, and Marcia Wallace, and so "at one point I thought of simply picking up the old show four years later. I think it might have worked."

For several weeks he continued to mull over the possibilities. Then "the idea hit me when Ginny and I were vacationing in a small hotel in the state of Washington. We used to sit around in the hotel coffee shop listening to the employees griping about the guy in 291 who cooked in his room, the old lady in 314 who never had enough heat, and things like that. I suddenly thought, 'Here's a way of doing the old show without doing the old show.' What I do best is sit and listen and react to what people say. As a psychologist in the old show, I couldn't tell a patient, 'You're nuts—get out of here.' I had to listen. It's the same with an innkeeper. The customer's always right."

At first Newhart wanted to use a large hotel for the setting. But when Newhart called in Barry Kemp, who had been the executive script consultant for "Taxi," to write the pilot episode, Kemp suggested something different. Says Newhart, "Barry Kemp . . . came up with the idea of putting the inn in Vermont, where we'd have the stubborn New England mentality to deal with, plus a lot of interesting historical background to play off of."

Kemp says that the bed-and-breakfast inn is "a current American fantasy" and that the New England setting "made us think about movies like *Holiday Inn, George Washington Slept Here,* and even *Mr. Blanding Builds His Dream House,* and then we began to wonder if those . . . two-hundred-year-old inns exist anymore." So Kemp went on a tour of small towns in New England—surely a grueling assignment by anybody's standards—to get a feeling for the area and to look for a particular inn that might be ideal as the setting for the show. Driving along Route 125 near East Middlebury, Vermont, Kemp spotted the Waybury Inn, which is the place we now see at the beginning of every episode of "Newhart." (He made a fine choice, for the Waybury looks as if it would make a perfect postcard.)

When Kemp got back to California, Newhart made several things clear to him. Above all, Newhart didn't want any children on the program. "We discussed doing kids in this show," says Newhart, "and then we realized we were going to be doing what every other show was doing." Newhart also wanted to make sure that the pilot script would be very different from "Fawlty Towers," the popular British situation comedy shown on public television in America. "With 'Newhart' I said, Let's not make it a "Fawlty Towers." Because, first of all, I'm not John Cleese—I'm not that physical a comedian. Secondly, I don't want to be accused of doing a rip-off. And, thirdly, I think that's an English form. I don't think there's any counterpart over here." In sitting down to write the pilot, Kemp's main task was to put together a new crew of oddballs whose zaniness would complement Newhart's dry style of humor.

Next, remembers Newhart, "Barry wrote a pilot script and sent it to my house. I circled the script for three days, like an Indian circling a wagon train, before I got up the courage to read it. By the third page I couldn't stop laughing. Barry had put in some wonderful things—like the fact that my character (Dick Loudon) wrote books like *How to Grout Your Bathtub,* had to deal with a bumbling handyman (George Utley) who couldn't fix anything, had a cynical wife (Joanna Loudon) he had to persuade to leave New York with him to help run the inn, and had this wealthy girl (Leslie Vanderkellen) who, out of some act of rebellion, was working as a maid in the hotel."

The executives at CBS and at Mary Tyler Moore Enterprises,

the production company, also liked the pilot script. Barry Kemp was made executive producer of the new series, entitled (surprise, surprise) "Newhart." The next step was for Kemp, who is also listed in the credits as the creator of the show, and Newhart to cast the pilot.

For the part of the not-so-handy handyman, George Utley, Newhart and Kemp immediately thought of veteran comic Tom Poston. Poston had worked with Newhart several times previously, on *Cold Turkey* and "The Bob Newhart Show." Before "Newhart," he probably had been best-known for his role on "The Steve Allen Show" back in the late fifties. On "Steve Allen," Poston played a man-on-the-street who always seemed to have trouble remembering his own name, and he won an Emmy as best supporting actor for 1958. During the sixties and seventies he was familiar to TV viewers as a panelist on "To Tell the Truth" and as a guest star on many sitcoms. (About Newhart, Poston says, "I think Bob is the funniest man I've ever known. I used to say, 'Steve Allen is the funniest man I've ever known,' but I don't work for him anymore.")

Poston brings a droll touch to his portrayal of George Utley that makes the character one of the best features of "Newhart." Poston plays Utley as the most phlegmatic guy imaginable. (The viewer sometimes wonders what it would take to get George excited. Somehow we doubt that even the announcement of the start of World War III would do the trick.) And even the way that George walks is funny: sometimes he sluggishly moves at what seems to be slower than a snail's pace.

The part of Dick Loudon's wife, Joanna, turned out to be much more difficult to cast. The trouble was, as Newhart points out, "the lady had to be as different as possible from

Suzanne Pleshette. I didn't want the audience to catch on that the new show was like the old show but in a different guise."

The producers saw about two hundred actresses before settling on Mary Frann. "The search for Joanna was one of our priorities," Kemp remembers. "We knew it had to be someone who played well against Bob. . . . One of our first impressions of Mary was her personality. If a show may run five to seven years, you want to be sure you know and understand each person. In Joanna's case, she was going to be up there with three people who, aside from being comic actors, were comics themselves. Whoever played Joanna had to be serious about her work, but not serious about herself. She had to be able to take it and dish it out. There was a lot of joking and kidding in our meetings with Mary, and she kept zinging us back. We liked the way she handled herself."

Newhart says, "Of the people we saw, she was clearly the best. She had never played much comedy, but she knows how to deliver a line. Every comedian knows that a good straight person is absolutely essential. Look what Abbott did for Costello, or Dean Martin for Jerry Lewis."

At the time she was cast on "Newhart," Mary Frann had had over ten years of experience acting for television, even though she had yet to become a well-known face. She was in the cast of the soap opera "Days of Our Lives" for four years, as well as appearing on series like "WKRP in Cincinnati," "Return to Peyton Place," "King's Crossing," and "Love of Life." Mary, whose given name was Mary Frances Luecke, had once been America's Junior Miss, and one of her first jobs after college was as a weather-girl on KSDA-TV in St. Louis—although "I didn't know a cumulus from a zoomaloop."

By taking the assignment of portraying Joanna, Mary knew that many of Newhart's fans would feel almost betrayed at the thought of his character being married to someone who was not played by Suzanne Pleshette. (And to make matters worse, Newhart accidentally addressed Mary as "Emily" during the taping of the pilot episode.) Mary was resigned to facing the inevitable comparisons: "I know I have to expect a certain amount of that [resentment]. Joanna and Emily are similar characters, and after six years Suzanne is obviously very much identified with that role. But it *is* a different show. It's not as though I were following her in the role of Ophelia, and you could compare the two performances. . . . In any case I knew that whoever played Joanna would be very fortunate, and I very much wanted it to be me."

Mary recalls that when she first began rehearsals for "Newhart," the directors and producers told her, "We're going to try something revolutionary—we're going to have a married couple who actually like each other."

"I liked that idea," she says. "I think people are tired of seeing couples bickering, putting each other down: 'Who's more clever, oh, how witty.' I think you can be witty and have tensions, and it can be based on love. I play the wife in a loving relationship who finds her husband amusing and is delighted with him."

The chemistry between Newhart and Mary Frann is an important part of the show—and they do seem to be at ease with each other. Moreover, it's important for the show to feature two levelheaded, well-balanced characters in the center of the action; otherwise, the zanier characters would have nothing to play against.

Stately Mary carries herself in a way that suggests a certain ladylike elegance. (Her striking features and honey blonde hair are also easy on the viewer's eyes.) We feel that it would be fun to play some sort of prank on her—and that she would be a good sport about being kidded.

"In many ways Mary has the toughest job in the show," explains Newhart. "She has to pour a lot of coffee and deliver a lot of exposition."

Unfortunately, this does sometimes lead to a problem: Joanna isn't given much of a personality. Her role is usually to be supportive of Dick, and that's about all she does, most of the time. And Mary Frann, though she has a warm, likable presence before the cameras, is limited as an actress. She's good at being genial, but she lacks the spunk of Suzanne Pleshette.

While the characters played by Bob Newhart, Mary Frann, and Tom Poston have continued to be at the center of most of what happens on "Newhart," the other characters have changed during the course of the six seasons of the show. The producers have never hesitated to replace or add characters if things didn't appear to be working well. For instance, Michael Harris, Stephanie Vanderkellen, "J.J.," and Larry and the Darryls were all missing from "Newhart" at the beginning of the first season.

Instead, the pilot script called for other supporting characters, such as Kirk Devane, the owner of the Minuteman Café before Larry and the Darryls took it over. Kirk, who was featured on the show during the first two seasons, has his charms, but he is also very egocentric and prone to telling lies. (In the pilot, Kirk introduced himself to Dick and Joanna by saying, "There's something you should know about me: I'm a habitual liar. And that's not true.") To play the part of Kirk, Barry Kemp selected Steven Kampmann, whose previous experience in television had been mainly as a producer and writer for "WKRP in Cincinnati." "Steve made me laugh as soon as we started talking," Kemp remembers. However, Kampmann still had to get past a tough audition with forty other candidates before he got the job.

Kampmann says that working on "Newhart" was "180 degrees" away from the atmosphere on "WKRP in Cincinnati," which was "frantic . . . like a campus fraternity." Instead, says Kampmann, the set of "Newhart" was a much more relaxed setting in which to work.

Another character from the pilot who disappeared later (and under some mighty unusual circumstances) was Leslie Vanderkellen, played by Jennifer Holmes. Leslie is a bright student from Dartmouth who's studying for her master's in Renaissance theology while she takes a job as a maid at the Stratford Inn. In her job interview she tells Dick Loudon, "I want to find out what it's like to be average."

In one of those strange transformations possible only on television, rich-girl-turned-maid Leslie Vanderkellen became rich-girl-turned-maid Stephanie Vanderkellen (played by Julia Duffy) in the second season of "Newhart." And so Jennifer Holmes was out of a job. She says that from the beginning she felt none too secure in her position: "When we started, I was too scared to ask anybody about anything. . . . Every day I thought I was going to be fired. It took everything I had just to get my knees moving."

With the cast finally set, the pilot episode was taped early in 1982. And Newhart decided to tape with a studio audience because "an audience guides and corrects. A laugh track doesn't do a thing. . . . When you use a laugh track with no audience, the quality of performance is lower. And you never know if a little piece of business really works." On the night they shot the pilot for "Newhart," the audience was responding so warmly that Newhart remembers that at one point he whispered to Mary Frann, "This is a hot one."

The pilot of "Newhart" does a good job of introducing viewers to some of the kinds of situations that they could expect to see in later episodes of the show. From the beginning there was no doubt that the main point of the show was for it to be a vehicle for Newhart's unfailingly funny reactions to whatever situations he might face. The details might be different, his name might have been changed from Bob Hartley to Dick Loudon, but viewers couldn't be mistaken that "Newhart" was mainly about Bob Newhart.

As the pilot episode opens we see Dick and Joanna Loudon entering the inn for the first time. The man who's showing them the place says, "Here it is, the Stratford, one of the oldest inns in Vermont. . . . They say James Madison once stayed here."

While Dick immediately feels that the inn is just what he was looking for, Joanna is hesitant. "We're used to Manhattan. Our friends are there, our whole life is there. . . . Not to mention your work—you're used to writing in a tiny little apartment."

Dick tries to come up with several reasons for buying the inn. He seems to be especially impressed with the historical background of the Stratford.

DICK: We're gonna know things about James Madison that we'd never know from any book.

JOANNA: Like what?

DICK: For one thing, he didn't care where he slept.

(Dick says this while looking around the inside of the place, where a lot of repairs and cleaning are obviously called for. All of the furniture is covered by sheets.)

After hearing Dick's arguments, Joanna is still reluctant, yet she agrees to go along with the plan when she sees how much he genuinely seems to love the inn.

When the Loudons' first guest checks in and signs the register, this scene occurs:

DICK: Just give me your John Hancock.

GUEST: Where?

DICK: Right there . . . under John Hancock.

Later, Dick has a telephone conversation with his first guest that sounds remarkably like one of the bits from his comedy albums of the early sixties: "Hello . . . Yes, Mr. Pomerantz . . . There's no heat in your room? . . . Maybe it only feels like there's no heat because you've got that big hole where the window used to be. . . . Have you felt the radiator? Sometimes it takes them a while . . . You don't have a radiator? . . . Do you have anything in the room up there that looks as if it might give off heat? . . . Your wife's getting a little steamed? . . . We'll try and get it fixed right away."

Toward the end of the pilot episode, Dick is to give a speech to the Daughters of the War for Independence, a small organization of Vermont women, about the history of the Stratford. In the meantime, Dick finds a letter revealing that the Stratford was a house of prostitution during the winter of 1775. Dick hopes to be able to conceal this fact from the women, but, to his discomfort, they are extremely curious to know about that particular period of time. So he tells them, "Since you're forcing me to say this: ladies, according to my information, in the winter of 1775, when all your ancestors were staying here, the Stratford was not so much an inn as a house of— let me put it this way—there's every reason to believe you may not be so much daughters of the War for Independence as daughters of the three-day-pass. . . . If you could read the letters I've read, you'd see that this place meant a lot to our fighting men. It inspired them to rededicate themselves to the war effort—sometimes after just a few hours." At first the ladies are shocked to learn this, but Dick apparently manages in the end to convince them that the Stratford performed a real service at a crucial moment in American history.

CBS executives were impressed by what they saw in the pilot, and the premiere of "Newhart" was scheduled for the beginning of the 1982–1983 television season. Still, Newhart was well aware that very few actors or actresses had ever become the star of a second hit sitcom. "The odds against having even one successful series are about the same as being hit by lightning," he told a writer for *TV Guide* in 1982. "I realize I'm asking for lightning to strike twice."

But the public's initial reception to "Newhart" proved to be a repeat of the reception to "The Bob Newhart Show." "Newhart" quickly moved up among the top fifteen programs in the Nielsen ratings, where it has remained ever since. Most TV series reach a peak in their early seasons, and then gradually decline until the network puts a stop to them. Not so with "Newhart," which has proved a model of consistency in the ratings, year after year. For instance, the show finished in fourteenth place in the ratings for the 1984–1985 season, in fifteenth place for the 1985–1986 season, and in thirteenth place (with a rating of 19.6) for the 1986–1987 season. Furthermore, this consistency was maintained during a time when the show was moved from a favorable time slot on Monday nights following the successful series "Kate and Allie" to a later time slot on Mondays following "My Sister Sam" and opposite ABC's popular "Monday Night Football."

Surely the main reason for the continuing success of "Newhart" is the American public's warm feelings toward the star of the show. Even though the supporting cast may change from season to season (or from series to series), Newhart's fans remain loyal.

Likewise, the critics responded very favorably to "Newhart" from the beginning. For example, Robert MacKenzie's review in the December 25, 1982, issue of *TV Guide* said, "We Newhart fans are getting older, but we're faithful. We know that a Newhart series will be funny, low-keyed, and perceptive, and that it will be about grown-ups. We know we'll get a break from gross sexual jokes, cunning brats, and the generally overheated atmosphere of most new comedies . . . [And] that's how it turned out."

The reviewer for *Variety* wrote on October 27, 1982, that "the series looks like a winner all the way. . . . Newhart's timing can work wonders with a wry line, and he was provided with ample material by Barry Kemp's script. . . . Ad agency types and other prognosticators about the 1982–1983 season have consistently picked 'Newhart' as a sure hit—and they were right."

"Mr. Newhart is at the top of his form," said John J. O'Connor, *The New York Times*'s TV critic, in the October 25, 1982, issue, "and that means comedy at its best. Without moving much, without shouting, Mr. Newhart can squeeze more out of an innocuous line than anybody else in the business. His is not a world of wisecracks. He is a master of timing and delivery. There is no nastiness or hip trendiness. He is simply very funny. Sit back and enjoy this welcome new entry in a very uneven season."

Those reviewers with negative comments to make were mainly disappointed that Suzanne Pleshette was missing from the new sitcom. Writing in the *New Leader,* Marvin Kitman said, "What really bothers me is the absence of Emily, Bob's wife from his previous series. Does she know that he has run off to New England with some blonde named Joanna (Mary Frann)? Where did he find Joanna, in one of his groups? Maybe Emily refused to leave Chicago for the wilds of Vermont. . . . I'm willing to give Bob's present wife a chance, but honestly, I think the network owes us some explanation." Kitman may have been admitting to an almost . . . well, unnatural attachment to a fictional character, but he did have a point. We feel that Emily Hartley seems to be a person out of real life that we would have liked to have known personally. And we're a little chagrined to learn that we won't be seeing her in any new episodes in the future.

Even though a few reviewers had some misgivings about "Newhart," none had anything negative, or even less than glowing, to say about Bob Newhart's performance. As Robert MacKenzie pointed out in *TV Guide,* "Newhart himself has never been better."

As "Newhart" concludes its sixth successful season, the thought must have occurred to many fans that Newhart might be beginning to get a little weary of the long hours, possibly ready to take things easy again for the next few years. After all, he quit "The Bob Newhart Show" after *its* sixth year. But Newhart says that he has no plans to stop doing his current sitcom anytime soon. "I'll stay as long as it's fun to go to work," he says. "Or as long as they'll stand for it." In fact, he now goes so far as to admit that he made a mistake in leaving the old sitcom when he did. "In the fourth year of that show, we did about five episodes in a row that I really didn't think were up to the standards that we had established. I tried to leave the next year, but the network said 'no.' When they finally let me leave, I had changed my mind—the show had improved—but I was locked into a situation where I had said I was going to leave. . . . I'm not going to let that happen again."

And there's something else to consider: "I've used up all the versions of my name. If I decided to do another series in a few years, we'd have to call it 'The.'"

11 | "NEWHART"

One day George Utley, the handyman at the Stratford Inn, hears that his boss, Dick Loudon, is having money troubles. Immediately, George takes out his checkbook and says, "Just tell me how much you need, and it's yours." Dick insists he doesn't need anything, but George keeps asking. Finally, to humor him, Dick says, "$25,000." "Gee, Dick, that's almost half of what I have," George replies.

Dick is flabbergasted to learn that none-too-ambitious George, whose salary is very modest, could possibly have that much money. George explains, "My room and board here is free. The only things that cost me money are my Beaver Lodge dues and my membership in the Tool-of-the-Month Club."

Dick can't understand why George doesn't use some of his money to treat himself to a few luxuries. (Previously, George's idea of a big purchase for himself was a pack of chewing gum.) Dick tells George to live it up, just this once.

GEORGE: But I can't think of anything I really need.

DICK: Half the fun of having money is spending it on things you don't need.

GEORGE: What's the other half?

George is skeptical, yet he gives in to Dick's suggestion that they go out on a shopping spree. Dick finds no end of things he wants to buy in the local stores; George, however, sees nothing that arouses his interest. (After all, what would?) Dick points out various gadgets to him, but to no avail.

DICK: Here's something that would be perfect for you. It's an electronic memo-minder. You can keep track of all your appointments.

GEORGE: Oh, neat. (He thinks for a second.) What appointments, Dick?

Later, Dick succeeds in talking George into going out to an expensive French restaurant with Joanna, Stephanie, and Michael. George makes a determined effort to have a good time, but eventually he's so upset at the thought of how much it's costing him that he leaves before the food arrives. At the end of the episode George explains, "I'm sorry, Dick, I tried to enjoy spending money, but it doesn't make me happy the way it does you. It sort of makes me crazy."

This is the kind of situation that we see time and time again on "Newhart." Dick Loudon, the sophisticated writer from New York, attempts to show the Vermonters that their way of doing things is backward or out of date or just plain stupid. In the end, though, we usually discover that the small-town people have their own brand of wisdom. They may not have a cosmopolitan point of view, but they do seem to have a practical knowledge of how to get things done in their community. Some of the most amusing moments in the series come when we get a chance to laugh at the hubris of Dick Loudon, who usually is confident that he can handle any situation much better than the locals. He has totally unrealistic expectations of what will work and what won't in Vermont.

For example, in one episode Dick is given the task of coming up with a way to raise money for the town library. Dick, who used to work for a New York advertising agency, sees this as an opportunity to come up with a "concept" for a new marketing strategy to raise money. He dreams up a plan for "adopting" books:

DICK: We make a list of books we want, and then people put up the money to adopt a book for the library. We'll make posters. I see Hemingway, Poe, Shakespeare in baby bonnets, saying, 'adopt me, adopt me.' This is great, it's starting to write itself.

JOANNA: Yeah, all you have to do is get a couple of backup ideas, and you're all set.

DICK: Backup ideas? Joanna, when you've been in the ad game as long as I have, you can smell a winner. Adopt-a-book: take a whiff.

Despite Joanna's misgivings, Dick is sure that everyone else will think his idea is brilliant. At a town meeting he presents his adopt-a-book plan by saying, "I have an idea that'll bring in so many books that someone will actually have to alphabetize the card catalogue." Nevertheless, Dick's presentation is greeted by a deafening silence from all of those present. After an awkward pause, someone asks, "What else you got, Dick?" The only reaction Dick gets to his posters is that he is asked, "Who are those ugly babies?" To Dick's evident displeasure, Joanna's simple suggestion of holding an auction is greeted with a round of cheers from all the Vermont locals. Dick wanted to do something complicated, yet all they wanted was something very humble. As might be expected, the auction winds up raising a decent amount of money for the library to buy books.

In his new sitcom, Newhart is provided with a good showcase for his comic talents. Surrounded by a group of small-town oddballs, he often gets the chance to react in his irresistibly amusing way to the other characters. (Says David Mirkin, one of the producers of "Newhart," "Bob is the best 'oh' man in the business.")

Though not as consistently entertaining as his old sitcom, Newhart's current show has had its share of memorable episodes. And it has managed to be funny without resorting to the familiar sitcom crutches. Instead of endless wise-cracks and slapstick, the humor is usually derived from how the characters interact in believable situations. "Let's just say we're not a high-impact comedy like 'Laverne and Shirley,'" Newhart says.

Unlike the wackier sitcoms, the action unfolds at a leisurely pace on "Newhart." Most of what happens on the show is, like its star, understated and low-key. Tom Poston explains that "Bob Newhart is a great believer in the idea that there are many people who haven't lasted in this business because they had a tendency to overdo things." And it's a safe bet Newhart will continue to insist that his current show remain true to his ideas of what a quality television program should be like.

Naturally, Dick Loudon is at the center of focus on "Newhart." In fact, most of the other characters exist mainly to bring out different facets of Dick. Like Bob Hartley, Dick

Loudon is an Everyman character—a typical, mild-mannered, middle-aged American husband. He's good-natured and decent, yet—like Walter Mitty—he has dreams of glory that he will never get to enjoy in real life. For example, in one episode Dick tries to pitch his big idea for a novel to his publisher—who reacts to him with annoyance rather than enthusiasm. In another episode Dick tries (unsuccessfully, of course) to work as a cowboy out in the West. And there's definitely a boyish side to Dick Loudon: he enjoys playing with gadgets, slicing the Thanksgiving turkey, and watching professional football games on TV.

Dick is also a man who is very settled in his routine. He tends to do everything in exactly the same way every time and expects everyone else not to disturb his regular habits. In fact, he's so organized that Joanna Loudon once says to a guest at the Stratford, "You'll have to excuse my husband. When he gets up in the morning, he checks off 'got up.' "

Newhart points out that audiences tend to recognize Dick Loudon as a guy out of their own experiences. "I think there's an identification with the character," he says. "I think that women watch and say, 'My God, that's exactly what Norm would have done.' And then the men watch, and think, 'Oh God, I would have done it just that way.' "

As a writer, Dick Loudon specializes in how-to books such as *Building Your Own Patio Cover* and *The Joy of Tubing*. Apparently, these books are a bit on the dull side, though he tries to liven them up occasionally with passages such as this: "The first time you apply accoustical tile to your ceiling is like the first time man conquered space." (Dick reads this aloud from an early draft of one of his books, and then says, "No, it isn't," and crosses out the offending phrase.)

Dick has written dozens of these books on home repairs, yet it's obvious that he has no real practical knowledge of how to fix things. Everything that he knows is based on book learning. For instance, at one point Dick tells George how shelves are supposed to be put up. George is apprehensive, but he follows Dick's advice anyway. And when George, out of his innate sense of courtesy, puts up the shelves according to Dick's instructions, they soon collapse.

For Dick Loudon, it's a dream come true to be able to run the Stratford Inn. He says he's always fantasized about being in charge of a place in the country. Moreover, it's the ideal setting in which he can do his writing. Since he enjoys his situation so much (and since his books have sold pretty well), he really doesn't care if the place makes any profits. As an innkeeper, Dick is clearly a very easygoing boss: no one could accuse him of being another J. R. Ewing, ruthlessly scheming to squeeze out every dollar by any means possible. What other boss, besides Dick Loudon, would tolerate a maid like Stephanie Vanderkellen, to whom the concept of working hard is totally unthinkable?

As the host of "Vermont Today" on WPIV-TV, Dick aims to put on a serious, thought-provoking talk show. Much of the time, however, the guests are serious to the point that they drive most of the local audience to switch channels. One week, Michael Harris, the producer of the show, tells Dick, "Look at these ratings. We finally got a whole number. We beat the unoccupied channels."

Some of the best episodes of "Newhart" deal with the inevitable conflicts between Dick, who resists making any changes in his show, and Michael, who is willing to do anything (no matter how sleazy) to pander to the lowest common denominator of the audience. Typically, Dick will go to the studio expecting a discussion with Edwin Newman, only to find that the guest has been changed to "the Unbelievable Jerry," who claims to be a psychic, but is blatantly a charlatan. Dick is so put off by Jerry that he finally tells him, on the air, "You're no psychic—you're a weenie." Of course, Dick is later embarrassed that he could have said something so utterly unprofessional on television. Michael, on the other hand, is delighted, and deliberately books some more guests for Dick to insult.

One of them is Dr. Miles Randall, a pro–nuclear war activist, who on the next week's "Vermont Today" says, "I believe we should have a limited nuclear war, blow a lot of the scum off the face of the earth, and simply start all over again." Dick at first tries to avoid insulting Dr. Randall (well played by Simon Jones, who was in the cast of "Brideshead Revisited"), but finally the temptation is too great. Dick tells him, "I'm not going to call you a weenie, even though you are one." The studio audience eats this up, and, naturally, Michael is jubilant. In the end, though, Dick insists that "Vermont Today" go back to being predictable and dull.

Although Dick is no intellectual heavyweight, he does see himself—correctly, we feel—as a brighter-than-average sort of fellow. He definitely feels he is more worldly-wise than the small-town yokels from Vermont. (And, it must be admitted, next to people like Larry and the Darryls, someone like Dick Loudon comes off looking like Schopenhauer.)

Writing for *TV Guide,* Noel Perrin pointed out that "it might not be too much to say that Bob Newhart is the ideal father. At least on this show ["Newhart"], he seems to have only the mildest of personal problems . . . which is how a child normally perceives a parent. Instead, he has all his time available to save others, to counsel and advise. Especially, he saves old values, old landmarks, young lovers. But like a true father, and unlike fantasy power figures like the Lone Ranger or the Equalizer, he can be fallible, and that is part of his endearingness. Infallible fathers are too scary."

In our youth-centered culture, Dick Loudon (and Bob Newhart) performs the service of making middle age appear to be an enjoyable experience. He may not be ecstatically jumping for joy very often—or even once—but he does seem to be having a good time running the Stratford Inn.

As he did on the old sitcom, Newhart has shown a remarkable willingness to share the limelight with his co-stars on his new show. The supporting characters on "Newhart" are given a considerable amount of attention—and the time on-camera that is necessary for us to be able to see them as more than merely one-dimensional. There are many episodes in which the spotlight is on Joanna Loudon, George Utley, Michael Harris, Stephanie Vanderkellen, or Larry and the Darryls. Sometimes we may almost overlook that quiet, mild-mannered guy, standing behind the desk at the inn, who is ostensibly the star of the series.

Joanna Loudon is on-camera nearly as much as her husband, and she plays a key role on "Newhart." She's a warm, understanding, well-balanced woman who devotes a lot of her energy to bolstering her husband and to showing sympathy toward whatever he does. On occasion, though, Dick goes too far and manages to get her angry with him; her fuse is long, but even she can be provoked. A good example of this occurs in the episode in which Dick's old girl friend from college, Diane Beckley, comes to visit the Stratford. Diane is every bit as attractive as Joanna, yet at first Joanna doesn't appear to be particularly jealous. The three of them have dinner together one night at the inn, and Joanna and Diane compare notes about their reactions to Dick, which makes him cringe with embarrassment:

JOANNA: What attracted you to Dick?

DIANE: Well, I think, his caring, his kindness . . . his legs.

JOANNA (laughing): You're kidding.

DICK: If you don't mind, I'd like to step into another dimension.

JOANNA: Honey, come on, we're just having fun.

DICK (uneasily): I know I am.

He tries to get them to change the subject, but without success.

JOANNA: What else can we compare about him?

DIANE: Let's see. Oh, I know: How did he propose to *you*?

When Joanna hears this, her mouth drops open; her round eyes grow rounder. It's obvious that she has never been told about this proposal before. Meanwhile, Dick is looking even more disconcerted than before. He briefly flashes a weak, toothy smile. He knits and unknits his eyebrows. Later, when they're alone in their bedroom, Joanna is incensed that Dick had concealed something so important from her. His explanation is that "this isn't the kind of thing a wife likes to hear about . . . at least judging from the reaction so far."

Joanna is clearly very much in love with Dick, but that doesn't mean she is oblivious to all of his shortcomings. She gets especially irritated at his lack of spontaneity. In one episode she chides him for being too stodgy: "Dick, tell me the last time you went to bed without having all your clothes laid out for the next day, or the last time you went to the grocery store and got something that wasn't on your list?"

To show her that he can be impulsive, Dick wakes Joanna up in the middle of the night one time and tells her they're leaving at once on a trip. "Where are we going? I don't know," he says. At first Joanna is startled, but she quickly gets into the spirit of things, and they head off on their "spontaneous" trip.

As might be expected, though, disaster strikes soon afterward: their car gets stuck and they wind up staying in a sleazy motel. (When they arrive, the motel clerk asks if they want the room "for the full hour.") Joanna keeps insisting that the experience hasn't been all that bad, but Dick is furious: "This *is* a bad time. This is the standard by which all bad times will be measured." Joanna has to accept that Dick is never going to be anything but what he is—unadventurous.

Joanna serves as a good foil for Dick most of the time. Yet it must be admitted that their relationship is not as dramatically interesting as the marriage in "The Bob Newhart Show." While the marriage of Bob and Emily Hartley seems very real, full of everyday tensions and anxieties, the marriage of Dick and Joanna Loudon seems too good to be true. Even when they do quarrel over something, the Loudons don't appear to be truly angry—instead, their anger seems a trifle phoney. Part of the blame for this undoubtedly must be charged to Mary Frann, and part to the scriptwriters for not defining the character of Joanna as clearly as Emily. Joanna is, we feel, a pleasant person, but also somewhat colorless.

George Utley is, on the other hand, a very well-defined character. He's not terribly bright, he's simple in his tastes, and above all he's imperturbable (if Joanna's fuse is long, George's is infinite). As a matter of fact, George is so placid that he even makes Dick look lively by comparison. George lumbers through the lobby of the Stratford like an old Saint Bernard on a hot day. Tom Poston certainly does a fine job of conveying George's stolid personality.

George plainly doesn't have a great mind, or even an average one, but he does seem to have practical knowledge about how things work. (Early episodes of "Newhart" often played up the bumbling side of George, though in the past few seasons we have learned that he is actually much more adept than he was originally portrayed.) As the handyman at the inn, George has had to face, and take care of, the day-to-day problems that Dick mistakenly believes can be solved by reading his how-to books.

Although he seems to be knowledgeable about his work, no one could accuse George of having any trace of sophistication about culture or about big-city life. Indeed, George admires Dick for being able to hold his own in conversations with the intellectual guests on "Vermont Today." Dick likes George, yet is very much aware that George is something of a country bumpkin. One of the best episodes of "Newhart" is the one in which Dick is sent two tickets for a party in New York that's being thrown by his publisher. Joanna can't make it, but George is eager to go along. Still, Dick hesitates to invite him because he's afraid George, with his lack of savoir-faire, will prove to be an embarrassment in New York:

DICK: I'd love to take George to New York, but I'm going to a very fancy, sophisticated party. I'm protecting him.

JOANNA: I understand. You're a snob.

George wants to go badly, and so Dick finally relents. When they get to New York, however, Dick tries to send him to *Cats* instead of the party. On the phone with Joanna, Dick continues to deny that he's being unfair to George. Says Dick, "I am not a snob . . . Joanna, stop using that word." When George eventually does get to the party, though, things turn out quite different from what Dick had imagined. Surprisingly, everyone else, including Dick's publisher, Ben, is amused by George's stories about country life in Vermont. Ben even invites George out afterward for a night on the town in which, George reveals later, he meets Woody Allen at an art gallery in Soho. At the end of the episode Dick has no choice but to confess that he's a snob.

Stephanie Vanderkellen (played by Julia Duffy) joined the cast of "Newhart" in the second season. Julia Duffy had been a guest star in one first-season episode and had so impressed the producers that she was soon made a regular. "We were all knocked out by Julia's comedic talents," recalls Newhart. "Not to say anything bad about the other lady (Jennifer

Holmes), who is a fine actress with a lot of experience, but Julia was just funnier." Julia Duffy's acting on "Newhart" reminds the viewer of the performances of those sexy comediennes from the thirties, Jean Harlow and Carole Lombard.

The character that comely Julia Duffy adeptly portrays on "Newhart" is a vain, spoiled girl who works as the maid at Stratford. For Stephanie, work is a novel experience, to be avoided at all costs. When she holds a broom, it seems as if she feels it's a poisonous snake that may attack her at any moment. When Stephanie breaks her toe in one episode, by falling off the second rung of a stepladder, a doctor tells her to stay off her feet. "Don't be afraid to let other people do things for you," says the doctor. To which Dick dryly comments, "You're really gonna have to drill that into her."

When, in the same episode, Stephanie tries to blame Joanna for her broken toe, Joanna says, "I was just trying to get you to do your work." "I hope you think twice about doing that again," Stephanie replies.

Stephanie adores herself; she seems to be lost in her own world. She describes herself as "every picture-frame's delight." When she speaks, there's a haughty princesslike trill in her voice. When she's feeling a little depressed, she acts as if she were facing certain death. For example, when she fears that she is getting her first pimple, she says, "I'm going out to buy every skin-care product I can find. And on the way back, I'm going to stop by a church and light a candle."

Her life has not exactly been filled with obstacles to overcome. She explains that "Mommie and Daddy liked to shield me from the ugly things."

Stephanie's family is eccentric, to say the least—very much

like those madcap rich people in screwball comedies of the thirties, such as *Bringing Up Baby* or *My Man Godfrey*. The Vanderkellens never cry over anything but the loss of money. When Stephanie's cousin Ned Vanderkellen dies at his one hundredth birthday party, Stephanie tries to share her grief with her father (portrayed by José Ferrer). Her father then says, "Stephanie, if you're about to say something intensely personal and intimate, please don't."

The only subject that truly interests Stephanie is herself—especially her smashing good looks. When her boy friend, Michael Harris, excitedly tells her about a new project he's working on at the television station, she seems plainly bored as she responds, "How exciting. What does this mean to me?"

Another time, she is given a job in charge of a group of Ranger Girls. She introduces herself to the girls by saying, "Why don't I tell you a little bit about me, and then we can open the floor to compliments."

Before appearing on "Newhart," Julia Duffy had been in a few soap operas and the CBS series "Wizards and Warriors." She says that she loves playing in comedies. "There are an awful lot of girls around who can make their eyes teary," she explains. "And I know this is kind of heresy, but when you play tragedy, it can only go one way. It's tragic! But it seems endless to me, absolutely endless, the things I can do in comedy. And I don't mean doing a character who just stands out there and tells jokes. What I'm talking about is when you can take an ordinary line and make it funny. Because, you know, some words are funnier than others, the rhythm is better. And the best thing is to be funny with no words at all. Harpo Marx is my idol." (Does Newhart know about this?)

Michael Harris (played by Peter Scolari, who starred with Tom Hanks in "Bosom Buddies" on ABC) is a perfect match for Stephanie Vanderkellen in that he is, in his own way, every bit as shallow as she is. Scolari does a real scalpel job on eighties yuppies. His character is totally preoccupied with the trappings of success—and, of course, with Stephanie, his "cupcake." But "Michael is a *failed* yuppie," explains Scolari. "He drives a Datsun, not a BMW. He dresses well, but he's never been as successful as he wants to be."

On one occasion Michael is forced to confront his limitations when he goes to New York for a job interview with a network executive. Michael apparently believes that shameless flattery is the key to getting ahead:

MICHAEL: I've always wanted to be a web exec. . . . And, believe me, if it turns out you're my boss, I'll suck up to you like nobody's business.

PRODUCER: I wouldn't want you to do that.

MICHAEL: Are you sure? I'm good at it.

Michael discovers that the network is looking for quality programs, and he is astonished.

PRODUCER: We can always use someone who can bring intelligence, warmth, and human values to television.

MICHAEL: You want that stuff?

When Michael hears that quality is now becoming a trend, he realizes he hasn't much of a chance of making the big time. Since Michael is an ardent fan of "Gilligan's Island" and "The Partridge Family," it's hardly surprising that his tastes would come into conflict with Dick Loudon's over "Vermont Today," which Michael produces. Michael calls the show "visual death" and is always trying to slip some mindless entertainment into it. He'd rather see Dick doing pratfalls than the usual serious interviews.

Michael speaks a dialect of his own which seems to be based on his idea of the way the "trendy" people are talking today. Some of his typical comments are: "Dick, access those brain cells," or "Do you need the writing on the wall to be in neon?" or "Overconfidence and self-absorption is the eighties attitude."

The producers of "Newhart" made a wise move when they decided to have Michael and Stephanie fall in love. They play off each other very well, and they are so enraptured with each other that when they're together they have to be reminded that other people around them exist.

Michael and Stephanie's relationship consists mainly of Michael groveling at her feet, praising her in every way conceivable. He knows no bounds in flattering her, and she, the ultimate narcissist, laps it all up. The subjects of conversation between them are strictly limited to cars, clothes, and Stephanie's looks. Alone, they talk baby talk to each other. After listening to an especially sickening display of their affections, Dick says to Joanna, "Oh, to be young—and not them."

One of the few times that their relationship is put to the test comes in a memorable two-part episode in which Michael goes out with Susan Polgar. (Susan is Michael's assistant at WPIV-TV.) The reason, we soon discover, that Michael is attracted to her is that she treats him considerately, something that Stephanie is too spoiled to bother doing. In Michael and Susan's relationship, she's the one who does favors for *him*.

When Stephanie finds out about Susan, she becomes so upset that she actually starts doing all of her cleaning around the
inn. Stephanie tells Dick, "Michael left blonde, perky, and
drop-dead gorgeous for . . . 'nice?' My God, whatever happened to the laws of nature."

Determined to win Michael back, Stephanie attempts to
force herself to become nice. There's a delightful scene in
which Stephanie, apparently under a great strain, fights back
her impulses to be rude. She says, "Here, first let me take your
coat. Michael, I've never done this before. Do I just hang it
with the others?" Michael is amazed by the "new" Stephanie,
and at the end of this episode they have this exchange:

STEPHANIE: If I forgive you now, will you make it up to me
later?

MICHAEL: Yes.

STEPHANIE: And will I ever have to do this nice stuff again?

MICHAEL: Maybe once in a blue moon.

STEPHANIE: And exactly how often is the moon blue?

MICHAEL: Hardly ever, Steph.

The popularity of Michael and Stephanie with viewers has
been such that some rumors of a possible spin-off series have
been circulated in the press. But Scolari denies that he and
Julia Duffy have any intentions along those lines. "I couldn't
do a better Michael without Bob and Mary," he says, "and I
wouldn't want to do it without them."

On "Newhart" we get to meet quite a number of secondary
characters, mostly residents of the town, but none odder than
the strange trio of Larry and the Darryls. Larry always intro-

duces his brothers by saying, "Hi, I'm Larry. This is my brother Darryl, and this is my other brother Darryl."

Larry and the Darryls (played by William Sanderson, Tony Papenfuss, and John Voldstad) were first introduced in the second episode of the series. The story for that episode required someone who would be willing to dig up an old grave, and the three brothers, who say they will do "anything for a buck," agreed to perform the task. In fact, they positively relished doing it.

The brothers, apparently a product of some sort of inbreeding, have a special fondness for anything that is loathsome. They look forward, for instance, to an evening of "catching fireflies with our tongues." At their restaurant, the menu features such items as "the critter of the day," which apparently consists of whatever animal they find lying dead on the interstate highway that particular day.

Tom Poston comments that "they revel in the unsavory, but they get laughs out of it. Nobody knows why. Amazing."

Barry Kemp sees them as "three guys sharing one brain, and Larry has most of it."

Newhart admits he's been astonished at the cult following that Larry and the Darryls have developed. "They have now become generic," Newhart says. "In companies that have a trio of known incompetents, people will say, 'Turn it over to Larry, Darryl, and Darryl and let them screw it up.'"

Although Larry and the Darryls may be popular with some viewers, their style of humor seems totally out of place on "Newhart." Indeed, their appeal is mystifying. When they make one of their entrances, it's almost as if we have mistakenly changed channels to the wrong program. They are simply too ridiculous to fit into one of Newhart's low-key situation comedies.

Another baffling point about Larry and the Darryls is their hillbilly accents, which might make sense in Kentucky, but hardly in Vermont. There are a number of details about the show that don't reflect an accurate picture of Vermont, but this is by far the most glaring.

The presence of Larry and the Darryls on "Newhart" is just one indication that the show is not quite up to the standards set by the old sitcom. Another indication is the large number of changes that have been made in the characters on the new show. The producers have tended to try things out, to adapt the show to fit what the actors and actresses can do well.

On the other hand, with the very best situation comedies, such as "The Mary Tyler Moore Show" or "Taxi" or "The Bob Newhart Show," the people who produced the shows generally had a clear idea of what they wanted from the beginning. They had many of the details worked out. With "Newhart," though, the producers had some good ideas—and above all they had Bob Newhart—but they didn't really know what they wanted to do with several of the characters. So the show has tended to stumble along, waiting to pick up bits of inspiration here and there, such as finding Julia Duffy to play Stephanie.

Still, "Newhart" has had quite a number of very funny episodes, and it goes without saying that any series with Bob Newhart as its star is going to be enjoyable. He can always be counted on to provide something much more sophisticated than most of what we see on television.

12

A
TRUE
PROFESSIONAL

Those who have worked with Newhart say that he is a true professional, a craftsman who can be depended upon to do solid work and who also expects those around him to contribute nothing less than their best. As a comedy writer, he has always maintained high standards, and as an actor he has been a model of consistency.

Newhart's attitude toward his work has been a businesslike one. We never read any newspaper stories about him making temperamental demands or threatening to walk out if he doesn't receive certain perks. We never hear him complain about how difficult his situation is supposed to be.

George Avakian, the director of artists and repertory at Warner Brothers Records in the early sixties, remembers that "working with Bob was terrific, especially because he was so unpretentious, so straightforward and down-to-earth. Always a regular Midwestern kind of guy. . . . There was none of the big ego stuff you had to put up with with so many other performers." And Avakian adds that "Bob never really changed when he became famous. He was quite simple and direct. What you saw was what he was. And he stayed that way."

"He was easygoing, perfect to work with," says James Conkling, the president of Warner Brothers Records in the early sixties. "Bob was in the same category with Nat King Cole, to my way of thinking. They were both very talented, and yet you could always rely on them to do their jobs without any fuss."

Conkling describes Newhart as "very pleasant and congenial, but he isn't an outgoing sort of person. . . . He's always hiding away in some corner of an out-of-the-way restaurant. He's a shy, modest, quiet fellow. I can't remember Bob ever saying a dirty word, on stage or in person."

Many people have characterized Newhart as something of a loner, but Ginny Newhart says, "He's just selective about his friends. He's awfully funny at home, but when strangers are around he clams up. I tend to jump into friendships; he sits back and waits, and is generally right about people. The few friends he has are very important to him."

"He's a quiet, thinking man," says Mary Tyler Moore. "And he needs privacy. I'm that way, too. The thing I can't believe about Bob is that he was once an accountant. He's conservative and well organized, but I just can't put an accountant and a stand-up comic together."

There does appear to be a contradiction somewhere in Newhart's personality. He almost seems to be two very different people at the same time: one who is shy and intellectual, the other who is outgoing and loves appearing before an audience. Newhart says he is also puzzled by this: "I am very quiet and introverted. Yet I enjoy getting up and performing for an audience. The minute the performance is over, I am an introvert again."

Nothing is as depressing for Newhart as getting a bad reception from an audience, yet "on the other hand, I can't imagine a better feeling than when they're having a good time and it's because of me. Controlling an audience like that gives you a real feeling of power."

Newhart says he's a happy man because he enjoys the privilege of making a living by doing what he likes to do best. He's discovered that acting in a situation comedy is what his talents are best suited for. "I think I've grown," Newhart explains. "Maybe I've matured a little. And maybe I've found out, in doing some other things—features and things that I thought I wanted to do, that I couldn't have done while doing a series—that what I really wanted to do is this. It's a question of knowing who you are and what you are."

According to Newhart, the job of acting in a sitcom is not a grind at all, and he says he can't understand why most actors complain so much about their working conditions. "On the old sitcom I came in at nine-thirty and went home at five. Four days a week. [Says Tom Poston, 'Would you believe ten to four?'] You'll hear people on 'The Tonight Show' telling about doing some movie, and going on and on about how rugged it was—and it finally comes out they got five million dollars for it. It doesn't leave a good taste."

Newhart appears to be an easygoing fellow, but he still makes it clear to the people who work for him that he expects them always to maintain his standards of professionalism.

Poston explains that Newhart's sets "are the most orderly in town. He absolutely insists everyone do his job exactly right and with the least fuss."

"Some stars thrive on trouble," says Michael Zinberg, the associate producer of "The Bob Newhart Show." "Bob's not one of them. Most of us want to work with people who make us comfortable. For Bob, it's a necessity."

When someone does cause problems on the set, Newhart doesn't actually get tough with anybody himself. Instead, he asks his manager, Arthur Price, who is also the president of MTM Enterprises, to wield the ax. "Bob himself would never get into arguments or confrontations," explains Dick Martin, the director of several episodes of "Newhart." "But he doesn't have to. He has Arthur Price. . . . If there's anyone around making unnecessary waves, Art takes care of them. Fast."

Although Newhart is not listed in the credits of his sitcoms as the "executive producer" or "creative consultant," he does take on the role of overseer of what happens on his shows. Occasionally he suggests ideas for jokes or he contributes a few lines to the scripts. But mainly he intrudes himself in the process of scriptwriting only in order to exercise his veto power. He will tell the writers not to go ahead with a particular idea that he feels, based on his experience, just won't work out. "I don't like to interfere," Newhart says. "I'd say ninety percent of what you see on the tube is what the writers wrote."

Just as his long experience in comedy has taught him a great deal about which ideas will work, he has also learned how best to prepare himself for his performances before the cameras. During rehearsals he tends to work in a very low-key style, not expending much energy. His idea is to "save it for the audience." While rehearsing, his focus is more on *what* he'll say rather than *how* he'll say it. Newhart has discovered that he usually does well on the first or second take, but he has trouble keeping things fresh if he has to repeat his performance over and over again. This helps to explain why Newhart's reactions on his sitcoms always seem so spontaneous—and also why his style of acting is better suited to television than to movies or the theater.

"Newhart always says it will work once you get out there. Just step through the door and do it," explains Steven Kampmann, who played Kirk Devane on "Newhart." "And he's right. He's absolutely right." Kampmann says the contrast between his own technique of acting and Newhart's approach made for some conflicts. While Newhart was laid-back during rehearsals, Kampmann was very intense, rethinking his performances from one day to the next. "It was rough at first," Kampmann admits. Eventually, though, he learned to relax more with the role, as Newhart had suggested.

Newhart feels that it's important that people should be having a good time while they're working on a show. He believes this kind of atmosphere will also help everyone to be more creative.

"We have a tremendous amount of fun every day on the set of 'Newhart,'" says Poston. "In fact, my wife came to the set one day and saw what things were like. And then she said to me, 'Don't let me ever hear you complaining again about how hard you're supposed to be working.'"

Poston says, "Bob is terrifically funny in person. He's always making jokes about what's in the news. He loves topical stuff. I'll give you an example: After Fergie got married to Prince Andrew, she was staying with her husband at Windsor Castle. Bob said he thought that Princess Di must have been nervous when she passed by Fergie's bedroom and heard her shouting, 'You're the king! You're the king!'"

Newhart agrees that he likes to comment on whatever is in the news: "Although I don't do personal appearances often nowadays, I still look in the papers for material. It's a habit from thirty years of paying attention to that sort of stuff. Recently, for instance, there was an interesting article about how the American University in Beirut is for some reason having trouble attracting professors. And they did a study and they found out two reasons. One was a fear of being taken hostage, and the other was inflation. Apparently, there's a runaway inflation in Beirut. And that kind of conjured up to my mind a guy saying, 'After this year, I'm quitting.' And they ask, 'Afraid of being taken hostage?' And he says, 'No. You have any idea what a hamburger costs here? How can you possibly save any money?'"

Newhart has always been willing to share the limelight with his co-stars on his situation comedies. "He's not one of those actors who count how many lines they've got in this week's script," explains David Davis, the executive producer of "The Bob Newhart Show." As a result, the other characters on Newhart's shows are given almost as much attention as the star of the series himself.

"Jack Benny used to give many of the good lines to Phil Harris or Mary or Rochester," Newhart says. "People told him he was giving all the funny things away. 'Yes,' said Jack, 'but I'll be back next week.'"

Over the years Newhart has received an almost embarrassing amount of praise, both from reviewers and from his co-workers. Here are just a few of these encomiums:

According to David Letterman, "Bob Newhart is one of the giants of American comedy, and is really a funny man to talk to."

"Bob is an extraordinary talent," says Julia Duffy. "He says he just reacts, but . . . there are shows where [he's] like Charlie Chaplin at his best."

"Strange thing about Bob," David Davis comments. "He works small, but he gets those *big* laughs. They come more out of attitudes than lines."

Mary Tyler Moore says, "I admire Bob so much, both professionally and personally. I was thrilled when I met him at a party years ago because I'd been a fan of his for a long time. He's a different breed of comic, much like Dick Van Dyke. They expand *truth* to achieve humor, an attitude I respect because it comes from reality and lives on forever, with unexpected little twists."

"Bob is one of the brightest, dearest, and funniest men," says Suzanne Pleshette. "He's funny even without a line. And I like his discernment. He would never do a joke for a joke's sake—it has to be real."

In a review for *TV Guide* of Newhart's first variety series, Gilbert Seldes wrote that Newhart "takes your intelligence for granted. The sound of good conversation and the atmosphere of mutual respect . . . are rare and pleasant qualities [for TV]."

James Wolcott commented in *Vanity Fair* that "Newhart wears well. His modesty has a rumpled warmth. And no matter how dour or cranky he may act in his roles, some part of him reaches out for company."

Such comments usually make Newhart uncomfortable when he hears them. After being highly praised, his typical reaction is to wince and say something modest like "I've basically been doing the same thing for twenty-five years . . . and getting away with it."

Still, he does admit that he now feels a certain confidence in his own abilities that he never felt back in those days when he was working as an accountant. "I know," he says, "that I can always write something funny. A dancer can break his leg. A singer can lose his voice. But life will always be funny and I'll always be able to write comedy, and lean back and say, 'Yeah, I still got it.'"

NEWHART'S CREDITS

RECORDS

The Button-Down Mind of Bob Newhart (1960), Warner Brothers, WS-1379

The Button-Down Mind Strikes Back (1960), Warner Brothers, WS-1393

Behind the Button-Down Mind of Bob Newhart (1962), Warner Brothers, War. 1417

The Button-Down Mind On TV (1962), Warner Brothers, War. 1467

Bob Newhart Faces Bob Newhart (1964), Warner Brothers, War. 1517

The Windmills Are Weakening (1965), Warner Brothers, War. 1588

The Best of Bob Newhart (1967), Warner Brothers, War. 1672

This Is It! (1967), Warner Brothers, War. 1717

Very Funny (1970), Harmony, Har. 11344

The Driving Instructor (1973), Warner Brothers, War. K-36003

MOVIES

Hell Is for Heroes (1962)
Directed by Don Siegel
Produced by Henry Blanke
Written by Richard Carr
Released by Paramount
Running time: 90 minutes.
Starring Steve McQueen, Bobby Darin, Bob Newhart, Fess
Parker, Harry Guardino, and James Coburn

Hot Millions (1968)
Directed by Eric Till
Produced by Mildred Freed Alberg
Written by Ira Wallach and Peter Ustinov
Released by MGM
Running time: 105 minutes
Starring Peter Ustinov, Maggie Smith, Bob Newhart, Karl
Malden, Robert Morley, and Cesar Romero

On a Clear Day You Can See Forever (1970)
Directed by Vincente Minnelli
Produced by Howard W. Koch
Written by Alan Jay Lerner
Released by Paramount
Running time: 129 minutes
Starring Barbra Streisand, Yves Montand, Bob Newhart,
and Jack Nicholson

Catch 22 (1970)
    Directed by Mike Nichols
    Produced by John Calley
    Written by Buck Henry
    Released by Paramount
    Running time: 129 minutes
    Starring Alan Arkin, Martin Balsam, Richard Benjamin, Bob Newhart, Art Garfunkel, Anthony Perkins, Orson Welles, and Martin Sheen

Cold Turkey (1971)
    Directed by Norman Lear
    Produced by Norman Lear
    Written by Norman Lear
    Released by United Artists
    Running time: 102 minutes
    Starring Dick Van Dyke, Tom Poston, Bob Newhart, Edward Everett Horton, Bob Elliott, Ray Goulding, and Vincent Gardenia

"Thursday's Game" (1974)
    Made-for-television movie
    Directed by Robert Moore
    Produced by James Brooks
    Written by James Brooks
    First broadcast on ABC
    Starring Gene Wilder, Bob Newhart, Nancy Walker, Ellen Burstyn, and Cloris Leachman

"Marathon" (1980)
>   Made-for-television movie
>   Directed by Jackie Cooper
>   Produced by Joan Barnett and Linda Otto
>   Written by Ron Friedman
>   First broadcast on CBS
>   Starring Bob Newhart, Leigh Taylor-Young, Herb Edelman, and Dick Gautier

Little Miss Marker (1980)
>   Directed by Walter Bernstein
>   Produced by Jennings Lang
>   Written by Walter Bernstein
>   Released by Universal
>   Running time: 112 minutes
>   Starring Walter Matthau, Julie Andrews, Sara Stimson, and Bob Newhart

First Family (1980)
>   Directed by Buck Henry
>   Produced by Daniel Melnick
>   Written by Buck Henry
>   Released by Warner Brothers
>   Running time: 104 minutes
>   Starring Bob Newhart, Gilda Radner, Madeline Kahn, Harvey Korman, Rip Torn, and Richard Benjamin

TV SERIES

"The Bob Newhart Show" (1961–1962)
   NBC, Comedy/Variety
   Directed by Coby Ruskin
   Produced by Roland Kibbee
   First broadcast: October 11, 1961
   Last broadcast: June 13, 1962
   Starring Bob Newhart

"The Entertainers" (1964–1965)
   CBS, Comedy/Variety
   Directed by Dave Geisel
   Produced by Joe Hamilton
   First broadcast: September 25, 1964
   Last broadcast: March 27, 1965
   Starring Bob Newhart, Carol Burnett, Caterina Valente,
   Art Buchwald, and Dom DeLuise

"The Bob Newhart Show" (1972–1978)
   CBS, Situation Comedy
   Created by David Davis and Lorenzo Music
   First broadcast: September 16, 1972
   Last broadcast: August 26, 1978
   Starring Bob Newhart, Suzanne Pleshette, Bill Daily, Pe-
   ter Bonerz, and Marcia Wallace

"Newhart" (1982 to present)
   CBS, Situation Comedy
   Created by Barry Kemp
   First broadcast: October 25, 1982
   Starring Bob Newhart, Mary Frann, Tom Poston, Julia
   Duffy, and Peter Scolari

INDEX